CAFES

LINE DRU
CARLO ASLAN

PRINCETON ARCHITECTURAL PRESS

Line Dru was born in 1957. She is a licensed architect and designer.

Carlo Aslan was born in 1953. He is a licensed architect and holder of the C.E.A.A., "architecture and mastery of public works."

——————

The authors would like to thank both the architects and photographers who so willingly supplied their documentation of the cafes as well as the publishers of Electa Moniteur who made the project possible.

They would also like to thank Guillemette Morel-Journel, Jean-François Drevon, and Reynald Eugène of the AMC review for their help and support and thank as well Claudine Colin, Marie-France Paulin, Marie Wood-Perraut, Monique Wilmet, Jean Cartier-Bresson, Alessandro De Feo, Angelo Ferlazzo, Miltos Thomaides, and Sue and Terry Farrell.

The authors have to thank most especially Valérie Vaudou and François Roubaud.

Published in English language by
Princeton Architectural Press
37 East Seventh Street
New York, NY 10003
212.995.9620

English Translation: Alexandra McGovern
Production Editor: Elizabeth Short
Copy Editior: Ann C. Urban
Cover Photograph:
© Stéphane Couturier.
Cafe Beaubourg,
by Christian de Portzamparc.

Special thanks to Sheila Cohen, Antje Fritsch, and Clare L. Jacobson of Princeton Architectural Press.
—Kevin C. Lippert, Publisher

ISBN 0-910413-66-5

CONTENTS

THE NEW ARCHITECTURE OF CONSUMPTION

Among the following pages are a number of unique cafes constructed over the last ten years. The category "cafe" includes here everything from bars to brasseries, restaurants to night spots. This selection, which transcends the seemingly well-defined genre of the cafe, has its own rationale, for we understand by the term any public place where one can, as an old saying has it, "*prendre du café et des liqueurs*" (enjoy coffee and spirits).

Naturally, this amalgam erases many differences that exist in our vocabulary. A pub, a wine bar, and a tavern all used to evoke, in spite of their similar functions, different worlds with social divisions of profession, income, nobility, or political affiliation. Today, if it still exists, this social division is less clear. All these nuances are subordinate to the same factor: the consumer. In addition, the diffusion of the media has brought about a leveling of tastes and has lifted certain cultural taboos between communities. In other words, the consumer has lost a little humanity to become an anonymous figure. This banalization of the individual by the economy has in turn modified the social relations that are woven around the cafe. They are now less convivial, less ritualized, and conform more to the immediate necessities of the market. So the "cafe hour," which had been a time stolen from the work day or from family time, has become—as in a factory or a business—a perfectly rationalized economic time in which money must circulate rapidly. The act of consumption is no longer merely a spectacle in which people show themselves, each in his own way seducing and being seduced, becoming once again recognizably "human" during his time off. Now a client may sometimes be identified by what he is consuming, be it a glass of red wine or a well done steak. This type of dehumanization, this banalization, has been accompanied by a uniformity in the appearance of the cafes which, in Paris as elsewhere, are often constructed in the spirit of "pre-fab" characteristic of the architecture of the 1960's.

The criteria that contribute to the reputation of a cafe (the quality of the service, good food, location, the prestige of a name) have been affected by an additional obligation: the attraction of the decor and the architecture. No doubt, in the famed spots of yesterday, this aspect had its importance as well, but never before has it been so necessary to resort to art, to a "signature," to revive the rituals of appearance and obtain social recognition.

Certain cafe owners have fully grasped this emergence of a public concerned with finding forms of representation adapted to their new values. By attaching importance to the choice of architect and valuing his role, they have, in a sense, challenged the architectural indifference into which they had for the most part fallen.

The cafes presented in this book play on a sense both of duration and of the ephemeral.

Certain of them are trying to take root in the city, renewing themselves through architectural practices whose origins date back to Adolf Loos (Museum Cafe and American Bar). Others envision a more circumstantial, haphazard relationship between the urban and the historical. These tend to succumb more to the incessant change of fashion as in Cafe de Unie of J. J. P. Oud in Rotterdam or Cafe Aubette of H. Arp and Theo Van Doesburg in Strasbourg, for example.

There are marked differences in the historic approach of those cafes concerned with the idea of duration. These differences derive from national or regional particularities, the environment, a more or less clear desire to renew customs, or, more concretely, from the climate, the materials, and especially the cost and nature of the project, whether it be a restoration, a rehabilitation, a partial renovation, or the creation of a new space.

From this point of view, seemingly different projects share the same spirit: they are trying to enrich the tradition of the cafe. Their novelty resides in the variety of services offered (the Gran Colmado in

Barcelona), in the desire to transform the cafe into a space "by designers for designers" (Barcellona at Rimini), or in the quest for an ideal, socially accepted model, often generating surprising architectures: the Parisian Folies of Bernard Tschumi in the Parc de la Villette (Cafe de la Ville), for instance.

Other projects seek rather to draw models from the past and adapt them to the present. At one point, this choice takes the shape of an archeological reconstruction (the facade of the new Cafe de Unie in Rotterdam). Other cafes propose an ironic cohabitation of an architecture laden with historic values and an ahistorical modernity (Demmers Teehaus, Ange Rouge, and Schwarzenberg palace in Vienna).

On the other hand, some cafes prefer to update old models such as the literary cafe or the "regular's" cafe, using new materials or a modern design or expression (Cafe Beaubourg in Paris).

Occasionally, the architect draws upon the intelligence of the client, inciting him to react as an individual member of a collectivity. The decor of these cafes sends one back to the sources of collective imagination (the fast-food Aquylone in Reggio Emilia) or, if the decor is stripped and reflective, back to the client himself (the Cafe-Bar in Frankfurt). However, this schism between historic and immediate times reflects a specifically European perception. In North America, a rapport with the past conjures up uncertain cultural models. Historic time becomes another expression of immediate time, and architecture, seeking origins it cannot find, reflects simultaneously an individual sentiment and a collective conscience (72 Market Street in Los Angeles).

In another genre are architectures that seem indifferent to the concept of continuation; they address only the instant. These ephemeral places are primarily targeting a fashionable clientele that demands concessions to its image (Diva in Glasgow).

But the architect may sometimes allow himself liberties with regard to fashion, either because he has himself created a "look" (Joe's Cafe in London, Manin in Tokyo), or because he uses fashion to the point of going beyond it with a criticality that opens the door to permanence—or, at least, to historic time (the two Zen restaurants in London).

Freed from the constraints of tradition, architecture can also become a field of aesthetic experimentation, beyond the fickleness of fashion. This freedom of action sometimes concerns a whole building, even a complex (the project for the restaurant Snaporazz in San Francisco).

Sometimes particular work is put into the passage from the exterior to the interior, from a space beyond the control of the creator to its opposite, an "overdetermined" interior space (Dance Hall in Nagoya). This overdefinition of the interior, often in a language particular to the architect, can become an act of authority over the consumer, exercising itself in the smallest details of the design (Mimi la Sardine in San Francisco).

Elsewhere, we see the omnipresence of the architect take on a quasi-messianic feeling, turning the cafe into a miniature representation of nature's elements (Rhapsody Cafe & Bistro in Toronto).

Among the examples presented here are similarities dictated by fashion. But fashion is never without some value; it indicates the permanent crisis of appearances and is therefore a category of an historic time.

This method of classifying places according to their rapport with history may seem arbitrary. We could have chosen other criteria, the quality of the architect, for example—both builder and designer. Or we could have fallen back on the nature of the intervention, distinguishing between creations, renovations, rehabilitations, and decorations. But we all know that places and creators resist the arbitrary nature of all classification. So let us raise a glass to them: cheers!

CARLO ASLAN AND LINE DRU

The criteria that contributed to the good or bad reputation of a cafe (the quality of the service, good food, location, the prestige of a name) have been constrained to include one more: the attraction of the decor and the architecture.

WHY THE CAFE?

1. Cafe Museum by Adolf Loos, Vienna (circa 1910).

2. Cafe de l'Aubette by Hans Arp and Theo van Doesburg, Strasbourg (1930's). The tea room, based on a model executed by the architecture school of Strasbourg.

Le grand café

An interview between Carlo Aslan, Line Dru, and Gilbert Costes, client for Cafe Beaubourg.

Carlo Aslan and Line Dru: Mr. Costes, what was the program for Cafe Beaubourg?

Our initial objective was to create a space whose quality was representative of our time. We also wanted to play against the presence of the Centre Georges-Pompidou, a place where one expends energy and tires oneself, by offering a place to rest, a transition space between the street, Paris, and Beaubourg.

What lead you to choose Christian de Portzamparc?

For this project we needed an architect who was sensitive to the decoration of interiors. I had already met Christian. I knew what he had built and thought it very refined, very reposing. I don't know exactly what drew me to him, but there was an affinity, an understanding—we spoke the same language.

Did you have a picture in mind of the perfect cafe?

I have always been impressed by the big cafes and the big brasseries. The atmosphere, the commotion, is attractive. One is drawn in by the crowd, one wants to see what's going on inside. Of course, I could easily have made salons, like the Florian in Venice, which I admire very much. But that idea

bothered me. Personally, I like large rooms. When I go to the Coupole I like to stay; I never want to leave—whether I am with company or alone.

What was the generating idea for the project?

It was to be, as I said, a large, comfortable space, modern and new, where one could stay a long time. I was also thinking of the profile of the clientele, especially of people attached to the life around the Centre Pompidou, people interested in painting, literature, contemporary artistic currents, and, of course, architecture.

Aside from this general aspect, did you orient the architecture around specific points?

We needed a space for the kitchen, for the offices, space for the business rooms. Then we needed to find a gimmick to get people upstairs yet keep them open to the scene, because I felt that an absence of connection with the rest of the cafe would not be engaging: one would feel isolated and would not want to stay.

Were these questions resolved in the initial sketches of the architect?

When Christian presented his first sketches and his model to me, he had already given animation to the upper part and made the stairway an attractive event. The bridge participates in this coherence as well, meandering surprisingly and continuing across the main space. I mentioned the clientele earlier: a

clientele who likes to see but who also likes to be seen, and the bridge is, in this respect, an attraction.

You mentioned Coupole. Architecture has had little to do with its success. The public has made the place and its fame. Don't you think that the clientele may be less at ease in a space overly marked by architecture?

I don't know why you say that. You must be thinking of the musée d'-Orsay where it is said that the architecture takes on too much importance in relation to its contents . . . You know, when I arrived in Paris, the big cafes surprised me very much; I didn't understand why they were so big and so populated. I began to notice they had a refined personnel, carefully chosen furnishings. By reflecting on these aspects, one ends up putting to work for oneself what is good in other places and avoiding what is bad. This means closely examining all aspects of the business, from the look of the waiters to the music, from the shape of a plate to the design of the cutlery. Only then can one add that little something extra that makes a place new. For my cafe, that something extra was the architecture.

You prepare pleasant surprises for your clientele: for example, those tables painted by well-known artists. Will there be more of such things in the future?

In a place like this one must renew one's youthfulness. I opened this cafe eight months ago: I put on a party for the arrival of these tables. In a while, I will no doubt do something else, but I won't talk about it yet. I like things to be concrete.

People like the big cafes because they don't change . . .

Personally I think a place has a definitive personality that is born with it. But this "personality" has to be polished because it may become outdated. I am not talking about Coupole; but here, if I don't bring surprises, my cafe could become crusty.

These are changes that do not concern architecture.

Yes and no. The painting will deteriorate, the furniture, the people, could change. The container is definitive, of course, but the spirit can evolve.

But you will always act without betraying the image of the original architecture.

I participated in the conception of this place. I worked in concert with the architect as much in the choice of the materials as in the distribution of the spaces. Therefore I don't see how I could "betray" a place that I contributed to build, to make possible. My spirit is in it, you understand?

Fashion evolves, the style remains

An interview with Gilles Derain, designer.

When one asks Gilles Derain to create an interior space or an architectural project, how does he go about it?

First of all, I determine how much it has to do with me, or rather how much I might lose. This question is primary. Unfortunately it is never fully answered because the fee system and the devaluating image of the architect dictate that the client never has to disclose the amount of money at his disposal. And, by not having to state his budget, he will balk at paying the full sum later. So, for me, I don't do a job like that, I'm not from the "Ecole," I don't go looking for prestigious jobs that don't pay or that pay poorly. It's a question of professionalism. An architect who infuses science with aesthetics, who tells the client where to put beauty in his home, the client has no consideration for, the client considers him a lost fool who only knows where to place a bouquet. No question, I say no.

Nevertheless, you have occasionally said yes.

It's true, occasionally. The first time I thought I was entering a sphere of reflection different from the base I usually work from. I was quickly disenchanted. I realized that I couldn't develop a global intervention because the imagination was bound to the price of the square foot. The finishings, for example, are of capital importance for interior decoration. However, when one arrives at the last phases of a project, money is lacking and the project flounders, at least from

my experience. Recently I agreed to do a boutique in Tokyo, but that was an exception. Not only did I make a phenomenal amount of yen, but the client let me fully complete my work. I made a model and put everything in it: the door handles, the light switches, the little stuff; I did everything in miniature. They had been expecting a blueprint. They were completely surprised and satisfied. Of course, there were some restrictions in the execution phase, but over all I was able to do it all my way. I did something it is practically impossible to do in France.

Is the model an irreplaceable means of expression?

Absolutely. I myself have a hard time reading blueprints, so the client . . . If you show a model, the client is stupefied. He gets down, he sees how you enter, where the clothes are, where the cashier is, what the materials are, the contrasts. Models are the ABC of architecture.

Don't you think that all commissions are conditioned by the imagination of the client? For example, with the cafes, one is less in the presence of a collective memory than of stereotypes like the "basco-bearnais" style.

With the cafes you have to know how it works, at least in France. Every person who wants to open a bistro has to ask for loans: from the wine merchant, from the beer merchant, from the coffee merchant. Each of these three loans has its own bank. The system is

perfectly rationalized: the architects are chosen ahead of time, forms and materials are normalized: the terraces on the street, the "onyx" marbles, the dutch chandeliers. It's corporatism; it's a closed circle.

Does this rationale extend to the furniture, the china, the cutlery?

A cafe is not profitable unless a couple works there 18 hours a day. That's one of the bases of the problem. Absenting yourself to go search out the nice furniture, the nice china, costs time! There are therefore specialized companies . . . that bring together all the elements. Rationalization extends to all this and also to the soft, spreadable butter, the coffee at so many grams, the slivers of ham . . . Everything is founded on this, and from it becomes mediocre.

There are exceptions, and nowadays they are more and more numerous.

There are, effectively, commando actions. Marginals have appeared on the market wanting to bring quality, and this phenomena is expanding. That represents a real interest for the designer, the decorator, the architect. If we focus on the chair for example, its design is doubly fascinating. First, a chair is a difficult thing to make; secondly, if it works, it's a break because cafes always need forty or fifty chairs, plus stock renewal.

Nowadays one is in a situation of double competition: not only to do

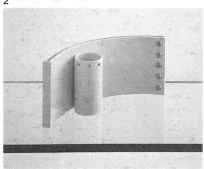

1. La Saladière by M. Mategot, Paris (1950's).
2. Ceramic vase by Gilles Derain.

better than one's neighbor but also to exist next to prestigious names like Hoffmann, Breuer, Le Corbusier . . .

You should not forget that the major arts have already said the essential fifty or sixty years ago, maybe even a century ago. You must understand that a designer is, above all, a great technician of forms. He works on synthesizing; he hasn't invented anything—he is fundamentally aside from pure creation. And never forget that what counts in design, as in architecture, is the aesthetic and, of course, the function.
But today, function loses its worth. There is so much competition in this business that pure function has been destroyed and design, or the "look," has taken its place. Now people buy for an identity of images, very little for the function; for example, one would gladly buy chairs that can't be sat in.
In the thirties it was the contrary: they said—I think it was Breuer— "He sacrificed form for comfort." What does that mean? That design and the minor arts are fashionable . . . and fashion is the slave of style. It always ends up oversaturated, submissive to dead people.

Architecture: as a style or as a tradition?

An interview with Francesco Dal Co, architect, historian of architecture, professor in the department of Urbanism at the Architectural Institute of Venice.

Today, rehabilitation operations are not all conservative. Some even pretend to define a new spatiality. Don't you have the feeling that this architecture within architecture augurs the spaces of tomorrow?

It can be that a rehabilitation project engenders new spaces, that it can be the occasion for spatial experimentations not allowed by the contemporary conditions of production of spaces. But I also think that we are witnessing a reaction against stereometry, elementary geometric shapes, the fashion of the prefabricated inherited from the tradition of modernism. We are at the end of a cycle, and everything that can contribute to the emergence of something new is probably useful. But it's difficult to tell now what that new thing will be, what will be the road it takes.

We were particularly thinking about meeting spaces like cafes, boutiques, places where fashion and "looks" are of primary importance, where "image" undergoes constant mutations.

Our society needs to produce images; it thinks it has to communicate in images. And architecture can absolutely satisfy this demand. It can do it more and more. Which is a sign that architecture is far from becoming a marginal figure in society. But at the same time this represents a danger, because a large part of contemporary architecture is already nothing but images! There are buildings, and not only in America, that are conceived, designed, and cut just like clothes and, like clothes, need to be changed often. What is the characteristic of style? To constantly change. And in America that now goes for architecture as well. There, the time for transformation and renewal of image is very rapid. Technology permits this to the point that certain architects have become fashion designers. There is not a great difference any more between Kevin Roche, Philip Johnson and Yves Saint-Laurent. They each make, in their own domain, works of disguise with the mask changing all the time. These are also masks that have no tradition, their *raison d'être* is the consumption of images. This expresses, I think, one of the realities of architecture today.

There is, however, some resistance. The reduction of architecture to the consumption of images is neither an irreversible phenomena nor a universal one.

There are, in fact, architects who wish to rethink architecture as an art, as a discipline concerned with preserving itself rather than renewing itself. It's true that there aren't very many of them, but they manifest a great interest in a practice of taking root that could react against this reduction of architecture to an image that must be permanently changing. This doesn't mean that they are doing historicist architecture. On the contrary! Historicism itself is an architecture of images. Postmodernism is the antithesis of the position of those individuals who are seeking a practice concerned with its own tradition and capable of producing images that find in something essential the will to last in time.

Who are you thinking of?

Many well known figures. I'm thinking of Aldo Rossi: the house that he recently built in Berlin is very significant. I'm also thinking of Stirling; and amongst others I will cite Francesco Venezia in Italy and Rafael Moneo in Spain. All these people are trying to avoid making architecture an object of immediate consumption. If you think of it, one of the extreme dimensions of architectural reflection is the project of a work conceived as a "ruin." This means, precisely, thinking of the real time of the work. But we live in an era when images cannot admit that; a fashion cannot think of itself as a ruin. It is always a novelty, even when it is very old. A fashion cannot have its own time. Well, we live between these two extremes. On the one hand, an architecture that is only images and, on the other, one that wants to last. If you look at it too closely this contemporary condition is disconcerting because it implies bad taste, immorality, a whole series of negative values. On the other hand, if you take your distance and observe this conflict attentively, I think it is very stimulating, for all periods with conflicts are stimulating periods.

On the social nature of pleasure

An interview with Giorgio Conti, professor in the department of Urbanism at the Architectural Institute of Venice.

The cafe, the bar, the discotheque . . . what is their place in the city and in "productive life?"

If the tavern represented in the Middle Ages a secular space in opposition with the church, the cafe in the 18th century represents in England the place par excellence for the economic and political elaboration of the industrial revolution. Today with a society of information spreading without measure, it is necessary to distinguish between the places of immediate meeting (face to face) and the structured space conceived for mediated communications (telematic networks). An ever more informal and immaterial system of production will have to be connected to the spaces provided for free time. These places will be multipurposed, telematic, convivial and—why not—ambiguous, which is to say open to the future without precise definition, transformable.

How do you see the intervention of architects in the shaping of these "ambiguous" places?

The role of the architect as a producer of identifiable spaces will certainly be important, but it may not be globalizing, which is to say "super-everything."
Personally I would hope that the project would be the result of multi-disciplinary work, an association between the sociologist of communication, the telecommunication engineer, the gourmet, and—in the area of new professions—the "maître du plaisir."

Is there, for you, a contemporary definition of free time, amusement, pleasure?

I think the considerations of Adorno and Horkheimer are still to the point. Adorno wrote on this matter: "Nature perfectly ignores pleasure, it only knows satisfaction of a need. All pleasure is social, in unsubliminated impulses as in all others." It is an illusion to think that there is such a thing as personal pleasures. It is society that orients, perhaps without fully determining it, the sense of pleasure of a period and of individuals.

Does there exist an economy of "pleasure-leisure," or does this notion have its own autonomy?

As Paul Virilio points out, after the "office towns" of the thirties there seems to emerge today the "joy towns" of the forties, the "game towns" like Euro-Disney at Marne-la-Vallee and Zygopolis in Nice, which are the privileged spots of social non-productivity. The risk would then be that the economy of pleasure would turn into programmed pleasure, automatic, cybernetic, leaving only a small margin to personal creativity and relations between individuals, encouraging instead the construction of a monopoly economy of post-industrial overprofit.

In that sense can one consider "interactiveness," of which the Fabriques multimedias du Plaisir are an example, to be an expres-sion of conviviality that goes beyond the economy or rather as one of its most refined expressions?

The social interaction of the future will combine more and more local and cosmopolitan dimensions, specificity and globalness, innovation and tradition. This interactiveness should offer ever greater possibilities for communication with a transnational vision, without borders, confronting lifestyles and non-dogmatic ideologies.
In this context, the cost of communication, the price to pay to establish the contacts or to establish the interaction of these "super states" of the imagination plays a role of discrimination for this dialogue-confrontation . . . Who knows? Perhaps the political economy of international pleasure is already being born.

LUIGI BLAU

DEMMERS TEEHAUS
VIENNA 1981

"A scream is an expression of despair, and this construction did not justify such an extreme."
Luigi Blau

At the beginning of the century, Vienna was at the crossroads of strong innovative currents. Art Nouveau, led by figures such as Otto Wagner and Joseph Hoffman, was trying to introduce a new architectural dignity to the capital of the empire. In his pamphlet *Ornament is a Crime*, Adolf Loos, foreseeing the war, attacked this ultimate attempt to impose on the city an architectural style that conformed so closely to the already ubiquitous bourgeois values. However, an alliance was wrought between the flowery building of Otto Wagner and Adolf Loos's somber constructions, leaving posterity a difficult (perhaps impossible) heritage to overcome. These two opposite expressions of architecture essentially cover the whole field of experimentation in forms and scale, from the object to the city, leaving only small

room for innovation . . . In Vienna, then, the architectural *tradition* cannot be discussed, because in the end, it is a tradition that accepts everything. Irony becomes a handy tool with which to work with history without feeding stylistic antagonisms. With this bias, novelty, or rather difference, reemerges in the city, reaffirming its rights over forms we thought were immutable. This is what Luigi Blau sought to express with a restraint far more suggestive than formal overkill.
The Demmers Teehaus occupies the ground floor of a *libre Renaissance* style building. In this peaceful order, Luigi Blau has introduced elements of Chinese composition evoking the world of tea. "In Europe," he notes, "tea makes one think of England; but for me, an English doorway would have gone unnoticed on this facade. Our culture has always been more sensitive to the values of the country of origin than to those of the colonial powers . . ."
The concrete expression of this

analysis is apparent in the design of the window frames, designed in a Chinese fashion, which support the exterior window panes. It continues in the materials put to work in the interior of the teahouse: teak on the surfaces and the trimming, red sandalwood for the structural elements. In addition, the composition of staggered rectangles that act as the partition separating the retail store from the tea room is an explicit reference to Chinese line. The overall effect borrows from elements that are typically Viennese, such as the Wagenfeld lamps and lesser-known materials such as the metallic beams supporting the joisting or the squares used to cover the floor. This meeting of two cultures produces a disconcerting space, but one which is absent of kitsch, because each language has kept its own autonomy. The mastered irony of Luigi Blau has left nothing to chance except perhaps the imperceptible relationship between Vienna and the Orient.

Location: *Mölkerbastei 5, Vienna.*
Architect: *Luigi Blau.*
Collaborator: *Thomas Fichtner.*
Work began: *January 1981.*
Duration of work: *10 months.*
Floor area: *185 square meters.*
Cost: *Approximately 175,000 dollars; 950 dollars per square meter.*

The first room is treated as an interior courtyard with the store and the beginning of the stairs in the back and the tea accessories in the foreground. In the top part, the mezzanine is used as a storage space; one can see the office behind the three quarter moon window. The floor is made from tiles by Sollenhop arranged in a motif of alternating smooth and rough squares.

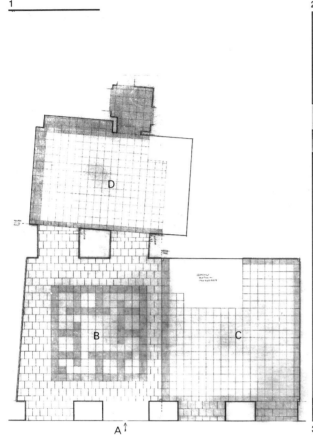

1. General Plan of Demmers Teehaus:
A. The entrance.
B. The interior courtyard and the accessories boutique.
C. The store.
D. The tea room.

2. The tea room from the interior courtyard. The open partition in staggered rectangles is mounted on red sandalwood. In the lower part, the shelves are covered in teak.

3. The stairs leading to the mezzanine and to the office. The structural elements of the furniture and the railing are red sandalwood, the finishing is teak.

4. The display window of the tea house shows a surprising mixture of languages: the classicism of the facade combines with the Chinese style wood framing. Through the window, one sees the Wagenfeld lamps, typical of Viennese design of the 1950's.

5. The two classical columns are deceptive. They don't indicate the entrance to Demmers but rather encase the window of the tea room. The entrance is signaled by the kitsch sign in the shape of a tea pot, ironically suspended above pedestrians.

6. Drawing of the entrance door and construction details.

7. Drawing of the facade.

COOP HIMMELBLAU

DER ROTE ENGEL (THE RED ANGEL)
VIENNA 1981

In Vienna, in a building constructed in 1835 by the architect Kornhaüsel, a metallic stem surges from the wall, passes through a broken curve and breaks into the main entrance. Two steel wings unfold, break the wall into pieces, and are frozen in the curves of the ceiling. This is the Red Angel; who, as the architects of Coop Himmelblau claim, animates the material with the voice of an actor, the tonality of a musician, and the breath of a singer.

The cultural upheaval brought about by the alternative movements of the 1960's has left its mark on the world. At that time people were looking for fewer conventions, fewer rules, and perhaps a syncopated representation of reality that would place one in a situation of permanent contesting. The return to order and to the work ethic, to the security of ideas that characterizes this decade, is being disavowed in this cafe-bar. As a symbol, the Red Angel evokes the vanity of all social order, imposing on it the sounds of the world, the unruliness and violence of cities, the profound and human vulnerability of architecture. But the typically urban materials that welcome the Red Angel's coming—the underlining of concrete under the bar, the asphalt used to finish the floor, the corrugated iron plaques used as wall panels and even on the doors—should not deceive. All these peculiar meetings are not the result of an explosion of values. They were pre-meditated and knowingly placed together. The rupture is artificial: the metallic bar piercing the glass is a perfectly controlled architectural event, as is the generous use of a broken line, making the space dynamic.

The collapse of the ceiling is eternally suspended . . .

The architecture is holding up, and one can partake at no risk under the sign of the Red Angel.

Location: *Rabensteig 5, Vienna.*
Architect: *Coop Himmelblau (W.D. Prix and H. Swiczinski).*
Work began: *December 1980.*
Duration of work: *6 months.*
Floor area: *130 square meters.*

The main room of the Red Angel cafe-bar. The wings of the angel are made of metallic beams and distorted bars covered with stainless steel. Between each "veining" the architects have placed clay mixed with broken glass. Shapes and materials are associated to underline the ephemeral quality of all architectural language. The concrete underside of the bar (hidden in the picture by the wood finishing of the counter), the asphalt floor, the corrugated iron behind the radiators are typically urban materials.

COOP HIMMELBLAU

1. Axonometric: the interlocking of the lines suggests the wings of the angel, which pick up and redistribute the load of the building after suppressing the internal walls.

2. General elevation for the Red Angel (top) with the drawing of the wings spreading, one towards the main room, the other towards the service entrance:
A. Main Entrance, 5 Rabensteig.
B. Service entrance.
Plan before the alteration (bottom): one can see the internal walls that divide the room into three small spaces. In the project, the architects eliminated them: the loads of the building are now carried by the wings of the angel.

3. The two "claws" mark the service entrance to the Red Angel.

4. The distorted bar of stainless steel indicates the impact of the Red Angel on the classical alignment of the "Rabensteig"; on the left is the main entrance.

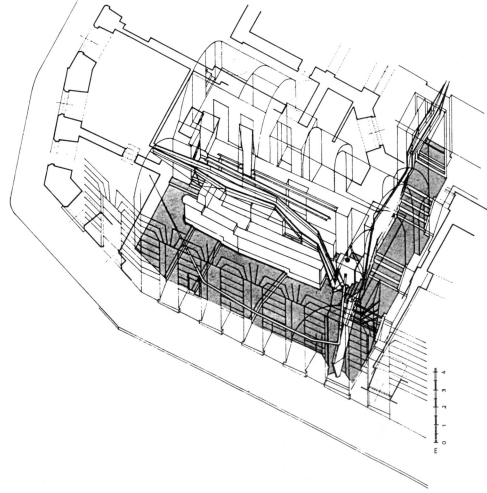

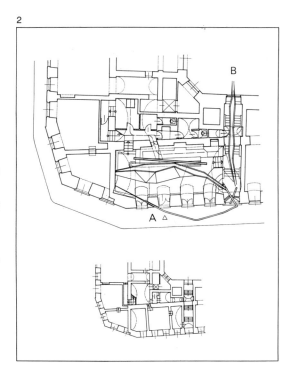

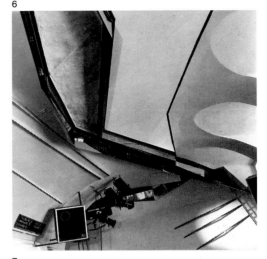

5. The pierced glass is behind the piano: the architecture defies codification and allows for the most unlikely combinations.

6. The wing of the angel meeting the original vaults: this scene occurs above the piano.

7. Preliminary sketch of the Red Angel.

HERMANN CZECH

SCHWARZENBERG PALACE
VIENNA 1984

"This light should come from underneath . . . "
Hermann Czech.

The prestigious, and therefore constraining, history of the building did not allow for any immediate action or preconceived ideas for the design of this hotel. "The departure point for the project was the architectural material in the building," says Hermann Czech. This required prudence on the part of the architect in areas where sensations, impressions, or suggestion overshadowed certitudes. Accordingly, banal terms like "drawing room," "bar," "reception," "armchair," etc., become for Hermann Czech "spaces in which one sits," "apparel rooms," "high shoulders and comfortable seat."

This desire to aggrandize the usual names of things is echoed in the lighting and acoustics, which have taken on a privileged architectural importance. These two vectors, which become indispensable for orienting the perception of the space, are an extension of the materials. They also regulate the behavior of the client. Consequently, the fabrics that cover the vertical surfaces absorb all echoes of conversation as well as exalt the carrying function of the vaults. In the same way, the choice of diffused light sources creates a chiaroscuro effect that flatters intimate conversations as well as the architect's furnishings.

However, this premise excludes neither distance nor criticism. On the contrary, it allows for a dissonance within the particular elements: the intricacy of the chandeliers, the emphasis on the furniture, and the brilliance of the varnishes are in contrast to the airy motifs of the carpeting designed by Christian Attersee. Extravagances become indispensable. The tapered awning echoes like a warning on the solid ease of the palace: its slimness seems to be a parody of the "narrowness" of a certain world. Buried under the certitude of its social recognition, slivers of baroque appear here and there as if to insinuate that a tradition is never innocent.

Location: *1 Messe Platz, 10-10 Vienna.*
Architect: *Hermann Czech.*
Worksite director: *Sepp Müller.*
Collaborators: *W. Gruss, W. Michl, architects; A. Heinrich, designer.*
Exterior collaborator: *Christian Ludwig Attersee, painter.*
Beginning of work: *August 1983.*
Duration of work: *14 months.*
Floor area: *5000 square meters.*
Rehabilitated surface: *1680 square meters.*
Cost: *Approximately 3,500,000 dollars; 2,000 dollars per square meter.*

One of the three dining rooms in the palace (no. 4 in the plan); in the back is the hotel sitting room. The walls and the ceiling are covered in colored fabrics. The lamps and the appliqués encrusted in the oval mirrors give off a diffused light that guarantees the guests intimacy without sacrificing the unity of the space. The ventilation grills play into the decor as well. They are inserted in the medallions above the two entrances. The airy motifs of the carpet, designed by the painter Christian Attersee, contrast with the pomp of the scene. Under the ochre of the arches, the gray of the walls, and the emphasis put on the lamps, the floor seems to slip away . . .

1. The Schwarzenberg Palace at the beginning of the century.

2. The jaunty awning, covered with fine stretched canvas, copies with flare the solid ease of the palace. As Hermann Czech says: "Where does the old end and the new begin?"

3. General layout for the basement level of the palace, with the transformation of the kitchens, the restaurants, and the creation of a bar. The reception room was not affected by the project.

4. Distribution corridor: the geometric pattern in the ceiling, the eccentric positioning of the lights, the design of the display cases, the cut of the floorboards that picks up on the floor's slight incline, the "manic" picture hanging, the artistic carpet . . . Hermann Czech has not left any loose ends in his project.

5. Study for the "crystal chandelier" based on classical and baroque motifs. Such a precious lamp is not only an aesthetic choice, it is also a good way to avoid dazzling light.

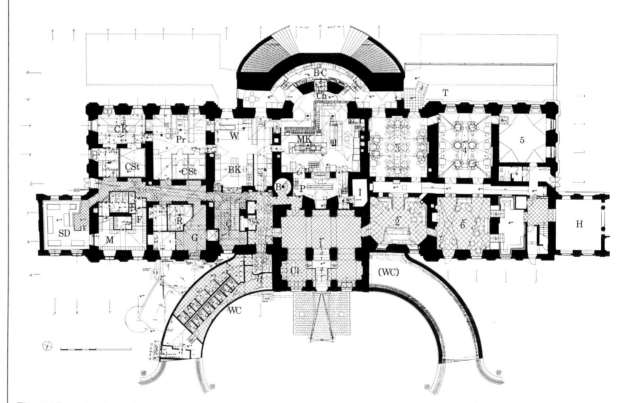

The public part of the palace:

1. Sala terrena (to welcome the guests).
C.I. Coatroom.
2. Bar of the hotel's restaurant.
3. Restaurant.
4. Restaurant reserved for hotel guests.

5. Private restaurant room.
6. Hotel sitting room.
H. Hotel lobby.
9. Distribution corridor.

(The offices, which were entirely rehabilitated by the architect, are concentrated in the part of the plan that is not numbered.)

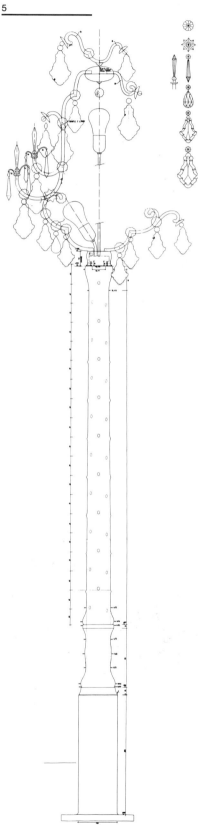

1. Restaurant (no. 5 in the plan), occasionally used as a meeting or conference room.

2. In the hall of the hotel (a part of the palace that was not worked on by the architect and that is not in the layout of the basement) is a chair designed by H.Czech for "seats" that enjoy comfort and for nice "large shoulders . . ."

3. The restaurant and hotel bar.

4. The entrance to the sala terrena.

3

4

PETER PRANGNELL

RHAPSODY CAFE & BISTRO
TORONTO 1986

"In other words, I want to build an elegy of chaos."
Peter Prangnell.

On the ground floor of an office building on Queen West Street in Toronto, in a semi-basement, one enters Rhapsody Cafe from the hall. The foyer area dominates the room, and a couple of steps down, six standing lamps project light on metallic panels that work as reflectors. These overlap like metal clouds, uncovering large areas of ventilation pipes.
The light sweeps over the metal, drawing strange shadows on it. In the long, narrow room the bar is constructed as an accumulation of detached pieces (leaning bar, bottles, coffee machine, even barman): it commands and organizes the space.
Once again, the light makes the objects vibrate, like so many personalities repeated in each respective shadow.
Peter Prangnell was guided by an anti-conformist—perhaps even anti-authoritarian—conception of architecture. He declares himself "hostile to lines of identification, which lead us straight to prison." Thus he composes an interactive landscape of objects suspended or laid down like so many signs to interpret. An inventory of the objects in the space reveals the intentions of the project: "masks and transparencies." At nightfall, the plexiglass shutters come out of "translucent masks" and close in front of bay windows from the original south facade, the sills of which are in white faience.
Little lamps positioned between the windows and the shutters indicate the thickness of the walls, which are covered by somber plywood panels. Along these shadowy lines the furniture detaches itself little by little.
The color outlines the shapes, showcases the discipline, and reinforces the play of materials. The lighting controls the rest of the decor.

Client: *Underhill Management Ltd.*
Location: *160 John Street, Queen Street West, Toronto.*
Architect: *Peter Prangnell.*
Collaborators: *Tony Belcher, Valérie Mould, Bart Szoke.*
Structures: *Keith Taylor.*
Electricity: *P.S. Designs.*
Engineer: *John Van Herson.*
Date of completion: *November 1986.*
Floor area: *304 square meters for the bar; 181 square meters for the room.*
Cost: *Approximately 338,000 dollars.*

View of the room. On the right, the bar: black ceramic with a Corian surface made translucent through underlighting. Across from the bar, echoing the translucent counter, are the plexiglass shutters, shown at the point in which each window materializes as a "mask and transparency."

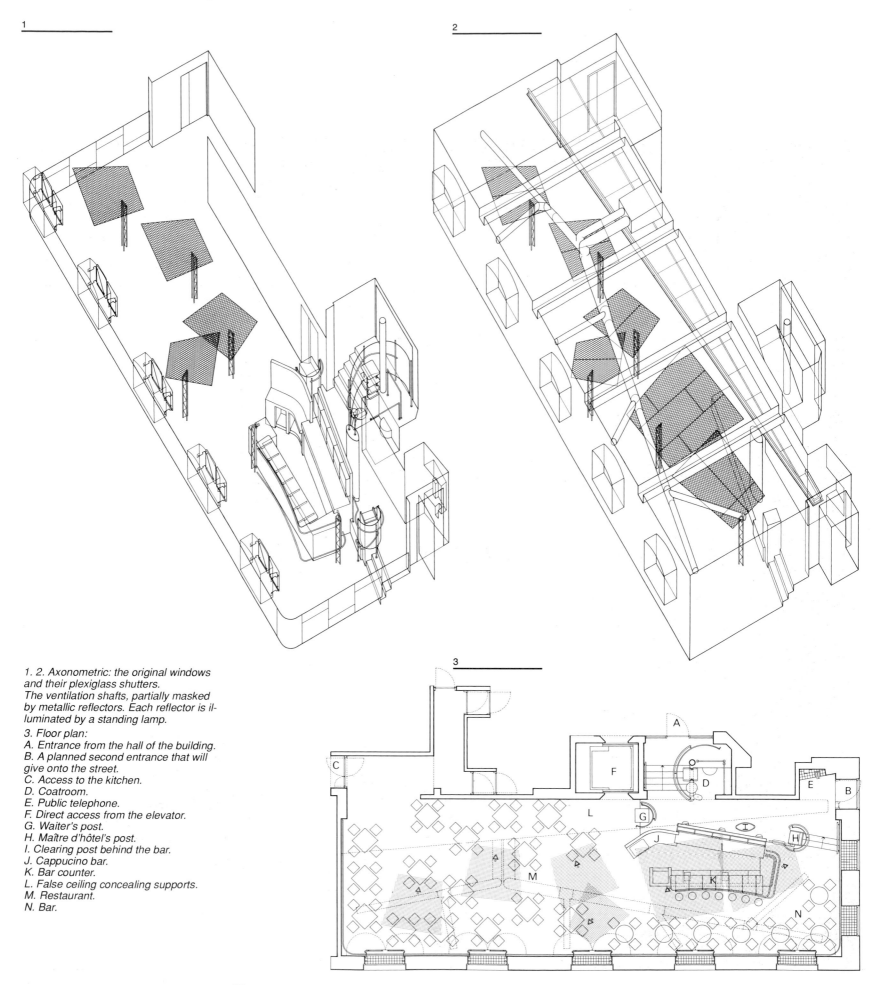

1. 2. Axonometric: the original windows and their plexiglass shutters.
The ventilation shafts, partially masked by metallic reflectors. Each reflector is illuminated by a standing lamp.

3. Floor plan:
A. Entrance from the hall of the building.
B. A planned second entrance that will give onto the street.
C. Access to the kitchen.
D. Coatroom.
E. Public telephone.
F. Direct access from the elevator.
G. Waiter's post.
H. Maître d'hôtel's post.
I. Clearing post behind the bar.
J. Cappucino bar.
K. Bar counter.
L. False ceiling concealing supports.
M. Restaurant.
N. Bar.

4. In the hall leading to the main room is a column designed like the wing of an airplane and covered in silver plating. The wall, covered in white faience, conceals the room and the bar service.

5. A panel of latticed metallic screening functions as a protective railing and delineates the coat room. The furniture conceived by the architect is made of tubes and painted iron.

6. Sketch of the bar: the top panel of Corian and the chrome support bars float in space, ignoring the alignment of the tiled bottom.

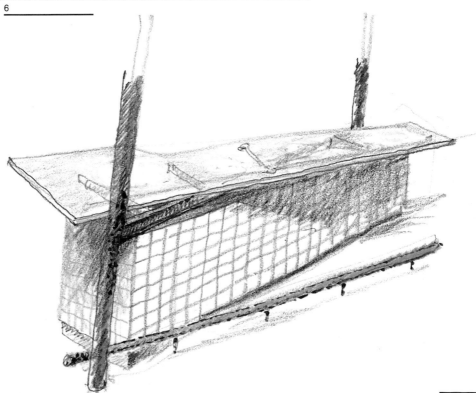

DANI FREIXES
VICENTE MIRANDA

COCTELERIA 33
BARCELONA 1986

Castilians, Basques, Catalans have at least one point in common: the daily ritual of the aperitif, usually practiced in small, smoky, aromatic places. There one talks of various things, rails on one's luck, perhaps, or maybe against the central government. In many ways, these Spanish cafes have been and are still a space of privileged expression of an indomitable urban democracy. Contained by the narrow limits of speech under Franco, democracy now explodes outward and demands a new look.

Cocteleria 33 seems to have been cut out to fit these new ideas. This location used to have two contrasting spaces. The first one, on the side of the street, had very high ceilings. Freixes and Miranda recomposed it lengthwise on a principle of autonomy for each element yet looking for an overall unity. So, among the service areas, the bar, and the entrance, a relationship was established.

Slightly elevated, the entrance extends the exterior space to the interior. This subtle interaction places the newcomer in the heart of the space. The theatrical effect is attenuated by the rounded shape of the bar, which invites one to take a seat in the depths of the room. This horizontal pushing back of the space is picked up in the vertical thrust of the false ceiling. Its diagonal cutout composes two triangles, one implied and one real and opaque. This points out the play between solid and space and also brings the volume back to a scale more relative to the lower, occupied space. The diagonal is repeated in the motif on the transparency of the door, contributing to the balance of the composition and creating a dramatic effect in the entrance. This balance, orchestrated for the pleasure of the eye, puts in value the mixed treatment of the walls (alternately smooth and distressed plaster behind which remains the stone), the dark panel behind the wall, and the variations in lighting. The ceiling, covered in mirrors, reflects the scene in all directions, accentuating the spatial extension.

Thus each architectural episode is given value, giving the space personality, a visual scale and coherence. Catalan autonomy, claimed as a true liberty, here manifests rights that were long denied. The number "33," composed of a "C" upside down and repeated, does not contradict this.

Location: *Calle Amigò 33, Barcelona.*
Architects: *Dani Freixes and Vicente Miranda.*
Collaborators: *Victor Argenti and Abel Curia.*
Opening date: *September 1986.*
Duration of work: *6 months.*
Cost: *Appoximately 46,000 dollars.*

The interior of the Cocteleria: the half moon bar, with the cutout triangle of the false ceiling, the dark vertical panel with the neon sign, the differentiated lateral panels, and the tiles on the floor. Each separate element communicates its difference by the material and the geometry in a surprisingly harmonious atmosphere. The volume is able to capture a warm and intimate visual scale.

1. The central space of Cocteleria seen from one of the lateral counters. The transition between the two areas of the establishment is indicated in the foreground by a step. In the background we see the two steps that indicate the transition from the interior to the exterior. Reflected in the glass from the front door, the number "33" reads as a jux-taposition of the letter "C," the first letter in "Catalonia."

2. Longitudinal cut of Cocteleria. The two areas are easily distinguished through their differences in height and the change in levels. Between the lateral counters and the half-moon bar (in black in the cut), a transverse passage has been created (in gray) not only to facili-tate the service, but also to underline the passage from one area to the other.

3. General plan of Cocteleria 33:
A. The slightly elevated entrance.
B. The central space of Cocteleria.
C. The two lateral counters.
D. The restrooms.
E. The patio.

4. The entrance to Cocteleria seen from the exterior.
Slightly off center in relation to the half-moon bar, the entrance reveals an interior that appears spacious from the street. The cutout triangle juxtaposed against the oblique imprinted on the door suggests a dynamic effect.

5. The half-moon bar seen from the step between the central and lateral spaces.

6. The contrast between the smooth counter and the coarseness of the dis-tressed plaster wall is sharp. The presence of a glass, however, is enough to remind one that it is just a theatrical use of materials.

1

2

3

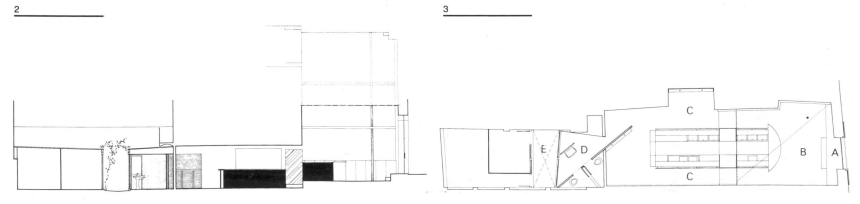

PERE RIERA

EL GRAN COLMADO

BARCELONA 1987

This *Grand Bistrot*, grounded in the depths of Barcelona, clearly and beautifully displays an array of fresh foods inside its shell of wood, glass, bricks, and steel. Its dimensions—53 meters long, 4 to 8 meters wide and 4 meters high—evoke the hull of a large ship with a cargo of sailors, spices, and dreams. The clarity of the supporting structure, the subtle gradation in space of the windows and display cases, and the plan itself all allow for the coming and going of the largest possible number of "passengers." The void is inhabited and reveals, in a composition of successive glass and metal shaftings, an impressive array of foods ready to be taken home or consumed on the spot according to the whim of the moment. At Gran Colmado everything is there to be seen, to be purchased, to be discussed. The high level of visibility is a guarantee of the quality of the product, its preparation, and the space that holds it. Nothing is hidden from view. As A. Vasquez Montalban, a famous regular, said: "Without looking to provoke, I would say that the main cultural improvement democracy has brought Barcelona has been the rediscovery of the pleasures of the table."

1

Client: *El Gran Colmado S.A.*
Location: *Consell de Cent 318, 08007 Barcelona.*
Architect: *Pere Riera.*
Work coordinator: *Francesc Serrahima.*
Collaborator: *Maurici Armengol, architect.*
Graphic studies: *Claret Serrahima, graphic designer.*
Opening date: *October 1987.*
Floor area: *500 square meters.*

1. From groceries to fully prepared dishes. Above, the walls, pillars, and beams bear witness to the building's past; below, the stainless steel of the cases, the wood shelving, the floor covered in glassified tiles or in exotic wood manifest a newness. The lighting points to this opposition between the new and the old.

2. The restaurant.

3. Plan.
The program followed by the chain of food stores also includes a library and an exposition space. This place disposes of a "subsistance" autonomy, which also reminds one of life on a ship.

2

3

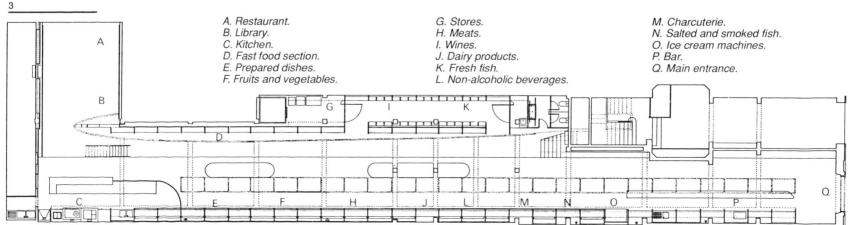

A. Restaurant.
B. Library.
C. Kitchen.
D. Fast food section.
E. Prepared dishes.
F. Fruits and vegetables.

G. Stores.
H. Meats.
I. Wines.
J. Dairy products.
K. Fresh fish.
L. Non-alcoholic beverages.

M. Charcuterie.
N. Salted and smoked fish.
O. Ice cream machines.
P. Bar.
Q. Main entrance.

GUILLEM BONET
ALICIA NUÑEZ
JORDI PARCERISAS

OTTO ZUTZ CLUB
BARCELONA 1985

Number 15 Lincoln Street is a building of unknown lineage. Its typology is familiar, however: it is similar to the large spaces with visible structural skeletons, peopled with giant machines, that are installed in the tangle of cities and have no contact with the daytime, indefinitely drowning in electric nights. But these are mere suppositions, subjective intonations that no one dared to "certify" until July 1985 when Otto Zutz, the revolutionary typographer, invested in these orphaned walls.

The aim of his "blitz" against the building is along these lines: to reinject into these pathetic reminiscences an atomic existence built on the consumption of fugitive encounters between initiates, survivors of a hypothetical urban disaster. In other words, to create a place well stocked with liquor, oozing coffee, and wonderfully smoky, where latter-day Robinson Crusoes can experience a new typography in a leisurely fashion, debate endlessly, exchange the final words on the individual or collective origins of music and, of course, dance.

This concept required a radical treatment. The architects first replaced the old wood frame with metallic beams and supports fixed to independent columns in order to facilitate work on the walls. This allowed them to build intermediary levels disposed around the central, gutted area and connected by a network of stairs and overpasses.

The space can no longer be grasped in a single glance. It is perceived in regular sequences, sparking curiosity to follow it in its meanderings. The stroller seeks some restful familiarity in the elements of the decor, but the alternating weave of the metal serves to make one feel more and more lost, especially since parts of the city appear here and there against gray backdrops, multiplying the references. The splitting of the bar into three distinct counters contests these points, none of which exert a dominant attraction. Each has its own personality, furniture, and fantasy.

The dance floor, made of squares of Brazilian wood with magical, superimposed effects, is the last resort to discover the secret order of the place. Situated in the middle of the labyrinth, it focuses all looks on the moving bodies, illuminated by blue, purple, or red lights. Spectators and actors are confused and form an undulating multitude that definitively erases the limits of the space. In this neo-Piranesian place, Buñuel's "exterminating angel" could start again on his work.

Location: *Calle Lincoln 15, Barcelona.*
Architects: *Guillem Bonet, Alicia Nuñez, Jordi Parcerisas.*
Graphic studies: *Pati Nuñez and Alfonso Sostres.*
Murals: *Vicens Viaplana.*
Lighting: *Guillem Bonet.*
Acoustic engineer: *Proser.*
Opening date: *June 18, 1985.*

View of the dance floor. The old spatial organization has not been modified. The architects simply replaced the wood skeleton with metallic frames in an "L" shape and a "T" shape. In the foreground, at the bottom, the beam that supports the mezzanine also functions as a stairwell and railing. On the right one can see the partition to the administrative offices, done in glass tiles. The overall space is awash in diffused light emanating from several sources and of varying intensities, depending on the needs. The spots of light reflected on the wood of the dance floor are from O. Zutz, conceived by G. Bonet. This powerful lighting is completed by stage lights and blinking lights. When it is dark, the stairs are identified by the points of light encrusted in the steps.

GUILLEM BONET
ALICIA NUÑEZ
JORDI PARCERISAS

1. View from the first level of the dance floor and billiard tables.

The dance floor is done in tablets of Brazilian wood, placed on a frame of young wood. The qualities of this exotic Brazilian wood are density, resistance, and elasticity. The wood is also covered with a resin that protects it from shock and renders it waterproof. The floor in the other part of the club is black poured concrete with aluminum dilation joints.

2. Otto Zutz's furniture: wood tables in organic shapes, with conical, black lacquered legs; wood framed sofas, covered in black fabric with light gray piping and brass tacks.

3. Longitudinal cut. The club occupies the ground floor, the second floor, and a part of the third floor. One can see the small arches in the ceiling characteristic of industrial buildings of the late nineteenth century.

1

2

3

4. View of one of the bars on the second floor; the mirror reflects one of the many murals that decorate the club.
The painter Viaplana executed all of the murals in two days, in the dark, with a broom. The papers on the rack were published by the animators of the club. They describe, in Otto Zutz's graphic style, the daily life of the club.

5. Otto Zutz billiard tables, in black, shiny formica with blue felt. The hinges are chrome.

JEAN-LOUIS GODIVIER

MIMI LA SARDINE
WALNUT CREEK, CALIFORNIA 1986

"How to reveal the image that the Californians have of the 'French spirit'" . . . Or, how to solve a problem without drowning in clichés.

Mimi la Sardine, the first link in a chain of American restaurants, has drifted far from its native French shores to an "artificial" city outside San Francisco.
In the hall of an office building in Walnut Creek, California, the architect built a restaurant based on the immediate recognition of the image of the chain and of its logo. An arc crosses the space, dividing what we see of the room and what we can only guess at in the annex rooms, protecting the bar from indiscreet glances.
Little blue glass lamps seem to float above the bar, suspended by almost invisible cables. Niches set between the cutout bays in the arc slow down the sweep of the curve. Around the bar, partitions folded like paper fans hide the service areas while, in the shade of a tapestry, V.I.P.'s vie for prominence in a private salon at the end of the arc, enjoying a meal they assume to be the daily manna of all rich and cultivated Parisians.
The slightly inclined ceiling meets the concave partition just above the bar. Square, black floorboards accentuate the curves and the partitions that mask the service areas.
In the tapestry—inspired by a freehand sketch of the floor plan—the logo is based on the same geometry as the design of the furniture: broken or curved lines structuring the space and imposing a unity. For the architect, the elements of the project "work in a syntax that not only directs the unity of the composition but also makes subtle references to 'classic' architecture and decorative ideas."

Client: *M. Suarez.*
Location: *Walnut Creek, California.*
Architect: *Jean-Louis Godivier.*
Company: *East Bay Restaurant Supply, San Francisco.*
Date of Completion: *February 1986.*
Opening date: *July 1986.*
Floor area: *300 square meters in the dining room and bar; 150 in the kitchen and service areas.*

The cutout shapes in the arched partition separating the dining room from the bar slow down the sweep of the curve. In the back of the room, a tapestry protects the "V.I.P." area; it uses the plan for Mimi la Sardine as its motif. The bay window is punctuated by black columns; treated like masks, they provide diffused light.

1. Plan and logo:
A. Entrance from the hall of the building.
B. Entrance from the terrace.
C. Bar.
D. Bar room.
E. Restaurant.
F. Private room.
G. Restrooms.
H. Kitchen.
I. Logo.

2.3.4. Crosscut. The arched partition hiding the bar from the dining room; but from all perspectives, the large cutout bay commands attention.

5. The bar area. The straight line of the bar, punctuated by the blue lights, and the arc of the partition across from it delineate the triangular space of the bar area.

6. The black, varnished floorboards underline the curves hiding the service area.

7. 8. 9. The cutlery and the furniture use the same geometric motif as the rest of the project: segments of arcs and straight lines that cross and penetrate each other.

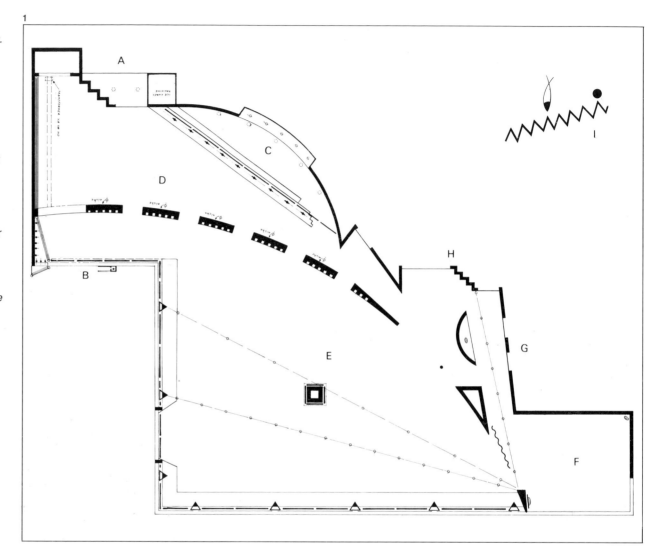

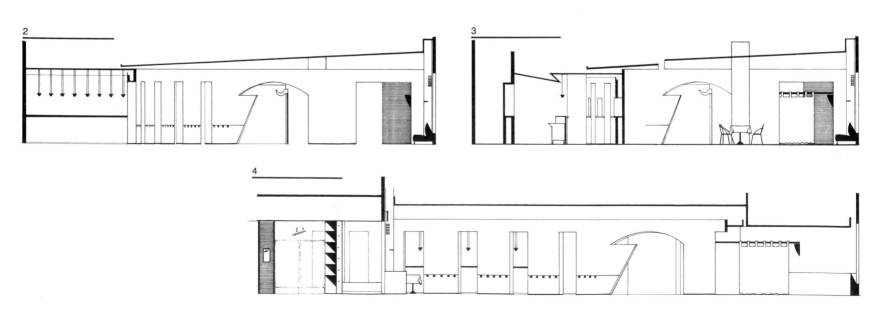

5

6

7

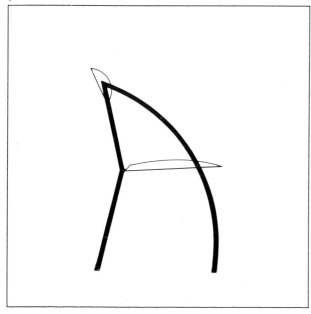

8

9

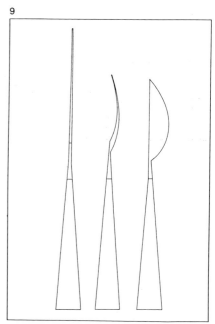

SOTTSASS ASSOCIATES

SNAPORAZZ
SAN FRANCISCO 1985

"To obtain the maximum range of sensory experiences."
Ettore Sottsass.

The restaurant Snaporazz was to occupy an irregular, accidental parcel of land—inscribed on a vast industrial stretch marked by slow change—lined up as an observatory of the San Francisco skyline across the bay. This site, which evokes the many movements that shake America, inspired Ettore Sottsass and his associates to put together a collection of custom-made spaces using a variety of materials. Brick is used for the exteriors; the roofings are alternately stone, marble, ceramic, or slate tiles; while steel, aluminum, and glass, the employments of which are easy and inexpensive, cover the "observatory tower." The coherence of the whole was to be created by the studied alternation of covered spaces, patios and terraces with custom-made paving, and "esoteric" gardens where one could eat, drink, and dance. However, this astonishing miniature did not seduce America. Snaporazz remains an unfinished project, a European dream.

1

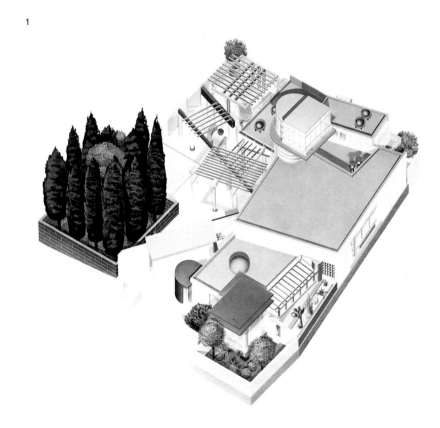

Client: *Douglas Tompkins.*
Location: *16th Street and Illinois, San Francisco.*
Architects: *Sottsass Associates (Ettore Sottsass, Marco Zanini, Beppe Caturegli, Giovannella Formica).*
Exterior collaborator: *Shiro Kuramata.*
Conception and presentation of the project: *1985.*
Floor area: *1589 square meters of which 786 are gardens.*

1. General model for the project. Gardens, terraces, and covered areas: between the interiors and the exteriors, a continuity of usage—for pleasure—is assured.
Each space has its identity, in volume and in architectural treatment as well as in the materials used.

2. Plan for the ground floor.

3. Axonometric of the patios with study for the paving, the colors, and the materials.

4. Cut of the main hall of Snaporazz with the temple gardens sequence, the temple salon, the "greenhouse" salon, the restaurant, and the service areas.

2

A. Service areas (prep rooms, kitchens, storage, freezers, restrooms . . .)
B. Placement for the observatory tower's metallic structure.
C. Main hall and main restaurant.
D. "Greenhouse" room.
E. Cocktail bar.
F. Circular room.
G. Temple salon.
H. Entrance.
I. Greenhouse.
J. Japanese gardens.
K. Temple gardens.
L. Meadow.
M. Marble garden.
N. Patios.

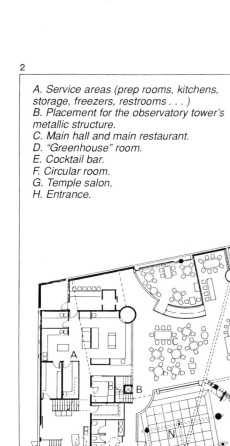

3

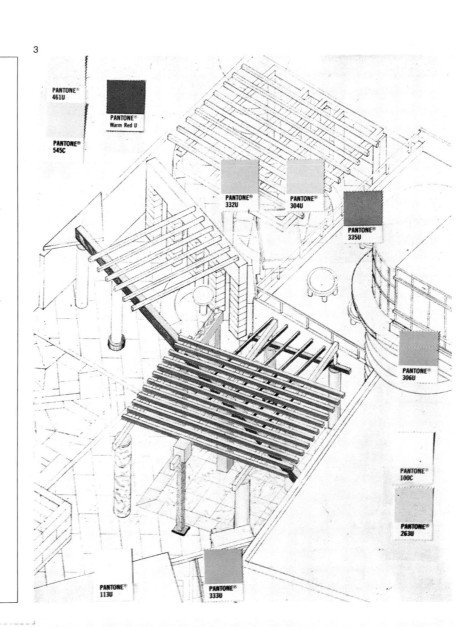

4

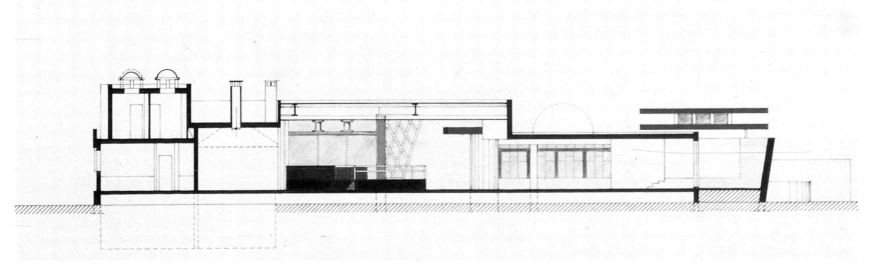

72 MARKET STREET
VENICE, CALIFORNIA 1984

Thomas Mayne— . . . An enclosed building that seems to fight to occupy a central position . . .
Client—Hmmm . . .
Michael Rotondi— . . . to repeat the original column; but it doesn't support anything, it reinforces everything.
Client—What?
(Excerpts from a conversation between the architects and the client.)

The actor-director-producer Bill Tony commissioned Morphosis to design a restaurant. However, neither he nor his associates (Anthony Heinsbergen, Dudley Moore, and Julie Stone) were restauranteurs. They agreed that a seafood bar was a must. But how to treat the problem of the presentation? The clients sent Thomas Mayne and Michael Rotondi on a long trip in search of ideas. The architects visited a good number of restaurants both in San Francisco and New York. At the end of the trip, Mayne and Rotondi served their clients a dish beyond their wildest dreams: a narrow street, often deserted, in a menacing environment—the seedy charm of Venice, California.

The first signal of this world is the patination of the armor-like facade. The only window, protected by a grill, is flanked on one side by mobile panels that allow the restaurant to open onto the street when the weather is good. On the other side, in the dent in the wall, the golden number indicates a chink in the armor: this is where you enter. Immediately, the original structure (whose bricks are still visible) delivers us its prey: a raw construction, pierced by large orthogonal bays, pivoting on itself, ignoring the axis of the building. In the center of this construction stands a totem-like pillar whose alignment with the exterior column, on axis with the door, suggests the meeting of several story lines. Absorbing the shock waves of the two confronting spaces, it is a symbol of gathering together. Taut steel rods connect the top of the cylinder decorated with human silhouettes to the corners of the hollow partitions. The light, streaming over the crossed beams and onto the walls, etches itself on the floor, like a projection.

In alignment with the window, a glass brick wall delineates a second room where obsessed gourmets can devour such things as cajun catfish.

Clients: *Bill Tony, Anthony Heinsbergen, Dudley Moore, Julie Stone.*
Location: *72 Market Street, Venice, California.*
Architects: *Morphosis (Mayne & Rotondi, architects).*
Company: *Pacific Southwest Development.*
Date of completion: *1984.*
Floor area: *316 square meters.*

In the back room, a glass brick partition rests on a small masonry wall of the same height as the tables; the glass allows one to divine the bronze pillar by the sculptor Robert Graham and, farther on, the only window, looking onto the outside portico.

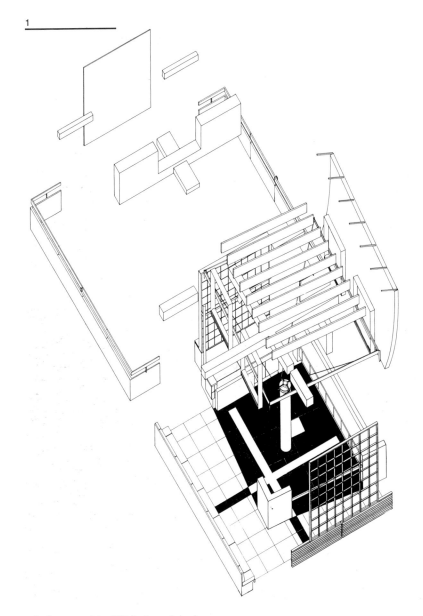

1. Axonometric. Within the original volume the new, unbalanced construction, whose raw partitions are pierced by large bays, defines an area marked on the floor by a change of finish. The window grill, giving on the exterior portico, replicates the glass brick wall on the inside.

2.3. The fortified facade is entrenched behind the 1900's arcade; the entrance is a hidden sliver in the blue patina of the antiquated bronze metallic finish.

4. Plan:
A. Entrance under the arcades.
B. Sliding panels.
C. First room: new construction and central pillar.
D. Bar.
E. Second room.
F. Service rooms.

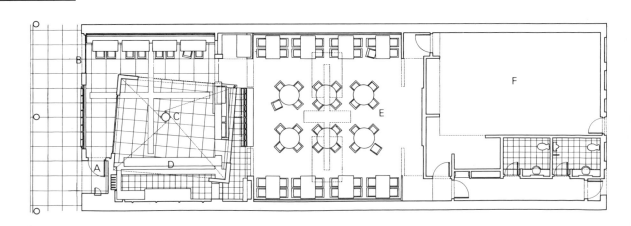

5. View toward the street from the first room: on the walls, the original brick is side by side with the tinted pine panelling. The opening of the window is regulated by a system of sliding weights treated like a sculpture.

6. In the first room, a bronze pillar decorated with human figures is connected to the new construction, pierced by orthogonal bays, by taut steel stems.

KAISA BLOMSTEDT

BULEVARDIA

HELSINKI 1985

Facing the National Opera, the restaurant Bulevardia occupies two stories of a building constructed in 1937 by the functionalist architect Arvo Aalto—less published than the more celebrated Alvar.

Over the years, this privileged location attracted all the intellectuals of the city. But the weight of the years and a general indifference to tradition had imperceptibly eroded the decor and the atmosphere of this brasserie: it had lost its soul. Only the tables were left as witnesses of the past;

the cafe's identity was sinking. Finally, even the last regulars of Bulevardia stopped coming.

At a loss, the owner considered turning his place into an English pub. Such architecturally cross-cultural references were in vogue in Helsinki and had already lead to several disfigurings, most notably Palace Grill and Restaurant de la Gare by the great Saarinen.

Enter Kaisa Blomstedt, who proposed a project conforming to the spirit of the place. With great respect for the original space, she

concentrated her efforts on the decor, the furniture, the accessories, the china . . . even on the menu. The interiors have regained their terra-cotta tint while the large balcony dominating the dining room is covered in thin sheets of elm. The generous lighting highlights the geometric motifs in the glass: sand blasted circles and squares.

This work, touching on scale and details, is a significant example of an "archeological" reconstruction of a modern building where tradition and innovation are linked.

Client: *Alexandre Zenkovitch.*
Location: *37 Bulevardia, Helsinki.*
Architect: *Studio Kaisa Blomstedt.*
Opening date: *June 1985.*
Duration of work: *6 months.*
Floor area: *(without the kitchens): 250 square meters or 130 seats.*

The ground floor of Bulevardia. Kaisa Blomstedt introduced new sensations: the mirror above reflects the return of the mezzanine and suggests the presence of an analogous space behind the lower opaque panel. The alignment of the ventilation plugs also accentuates the depths of the space. The terra-cotta color of the interiors, certain materials like the elm panels of the mezzanine, the worked glass, and the design of the furniture are in the spirit of the Finnish functionalism of the 1930's. These are the original tables, but the chairs were designed by the Finnish designer Jouko Jarvisalo. Johanna Blomstedt created the sandblasted geometric motifs in the windows. The other elements of the decor (the benches, the lamps, the appliqués, even the menu) were all designed by Kaisa Blomstedt.

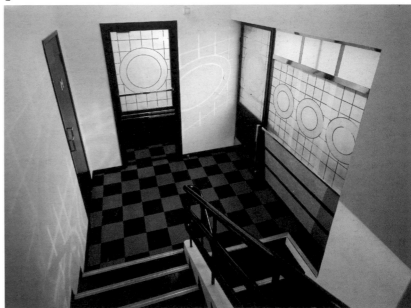

1. *View from the mezzanine.*

2. *The service stairway with access to the kitchen and to the service restrooms. As in the main dining room, the windows have been sandblasted.*

3. *The Kaisa Blomstedt benches, with the mezzanine overhead and the mirror.*

4. *Plan of the ground floor:*
A. Kitchen.
B. Dining room.
C. Main staircase.
D. Service staircase.
E. Entrance.
Plan of the mezzanine:
A. Dining room.
B. Private salons.
C. Open area over the ground floor.

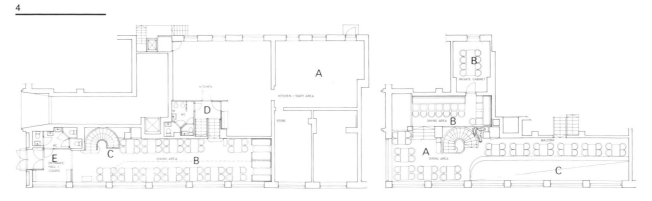

5. Main staircase of Bulevardia.

6. Half-moon furniture designed by
Kaisa Blomstedt.

7. Cut of Bulevardia: in the foreground is
the main stairway leading to the private
salons.

CHRISTIAN DE PORTZAMPARC

CAFE BEAUBOURG
PARIS 1986

"Finally I noticed, without really wanting to, that basically you always end up repeating the same project. In Cafe Beaubourg what counts is the people and the life around it . . ."
Christian de Portzamparc.

One could say that the function of the facade of Cafe Beaubourg seems to be to integrate itself with the buildings around it. Relatively discreet, it does not reveal its interior features. However, once the threshold is crossed, one senses the existence of more private areas beyond the deployment of the two-storied main space, like wings backstage.

At the back of the cafe, against smooth stone, fragments of a mirror surreptitiously reflect a glass emptying or the passage of a waiter. These shards upset the regular disposition of empty square holes, at the back of which is stretched sound absorbant fabric.
Eight columns covered in white stone from Spain define a two-leveled central area in this peaceful place. The visitor lingers, hesitates, ascends the staircase turned towards the light filtering from the ceiling. One flight up a calmer space opens: a mezzanine circles the central open area that is emphasized by the

delicate bridge that crosses it. The latter becomes the center of attention when an elegant woman passes across it. The wood framing around the windows on the mezzanine, the picture lamps, and the round table tops painted by sixteen contemporary artists evoke the atmosphere of a literary cafe. The low setting of the windows offers views from the second floor onto the pedestrian streets below, the Centre Beaubourg, and its animated square. The thick panes filter the noise from the outside; the constant agitation of the neighborhood does not disturb the tranquility of the spot.

Client: *Gilbert Costes.*
Location: *43-45 rue Saint Merri, 75004 Paris.*
Architect: *Christian de Portzamparc.*
Collaborator: *Bruno Barbot.*
Masonry: *Bouygues.*
Locksmith: *Supeljack.*
Carpentry: *Vaillant et Legrand.*
Plumbing: *Balas et Mahey.*
Date of completion: *February 1986.*
Floor area: *420 square meters.*
Cost: *Approximately 3,000 dollars per square meter.*

On the ground floor of Cafe Beaubourg the floor of the main room is covered in white granite, shot through with little arrows of Mexican blue stone, running between aisles of brown, "old fashioned" tiles.
On the back wall, a weaving of little hollow squares, fragments of mirrors, and sheets of text punctuate the smooth, fleshy stone. Two large bays span both levels, leading the eye beyond the partition.
The furniture was specially conceived by the architect: the table tops pick up the motif on the floor in the central area, the Bandar Log chairs are wooden on the ground floor and metal on the second floor.

1. With a total height of 5.30 meters, the ceiling diffuses artificial light on the central open space, which moves with the rhythm of the columns. The sightline is completed by a wall decorated with a fresco. On either side of it a fine surface of wood is stretched tight like a drum to absorb sound.
On the second floor, the transparent balustrade allows great visibility.

2. Plan of the mezzanine:
A. Empty area open on the ground floor.
B. Mezzanine.
C. Set back room.
The voluntary non-alignment of the central space in relation to the facades allows the architect to play with close or far perspectives depending on where one places oneself.

3. Transverse section.
Cafe Beaubourg was built following a rhythm of eight columns—steel pillars covered with 1.50 meter shells of white Spanish stone—which define a large central area bordered by aisles and balconies.

4. 5. 6. The entasis of the columns, the ascending spiral of the concrete staircase, and the "stride" of the footbridge give the place a feeling of circular movement underlined by the delicate curves of the chrome handrails on the stairway.

1

2

3

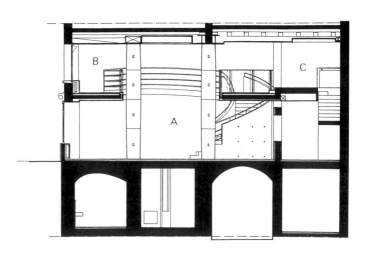

4

5

6

JEAN-MICHEL WILMOTTE

CAFE FLEURIOT
NANTES 1986

"What I like to do is to deform, modify, transform the base materials."
Jean-Michel Wilmotte.

This attitude engenders a worried spirit where the stress of creativity is stronger than the facility of repetition. The only thing taken for granted about a lamp, a chair, or a decor are the words that designate them. The shape must remain free, almost without definition, as if the architecture were escaping all oral or written expression. In the same way the conception of the space and the objects within it obey rules that are constantly questioned and allow all adaptations to continually change situations. You can recognize this process of "decomposition-recomposition" in the interiors of Fleuriot. Each element of the space—from the varnished wood finish of the walls to the worked glass screens, from the exposed guard rail on the stairs to the oval pillars of the bar, from the furniture to other accessories such as the venetian blinds—asserts its independence and its link to the whole.
Thus takes shape an architecture of joints where straight lines, curves, angles, and the open and closed areas that form each event manifest equally their constructive value.

1

Client: "La Jouvence" Society.
Location: Fleuriot-de-l'Angle Square, 44000 Nantes.
Architect: Jean-Michel Wilmotte.
Company: Etablissement Dupuch, Satra Society, Soning Society.
Opening date: December 1986.
Floor area: 300 square meters.

1. The first floor of Cafe Fleuriot.
2. The veins of the wood finish enclose the circle of the bay windows. The blinds slide over the glass and modulate one's perception of the world outside. The width of the sills detach the natural surface of the wood from the artificial blinds. The lines of the angles compose a symmetry and give this corner its spatial structure.
3,4. The stairway with marble steps, against one of the oval pillars that frame the bar. Its balustrade is of wood covered with black epoxy as are the elements of the chairs and the legs of the tables.
5. With a light touch, Jean-Michel Wilmotte prefers to let the materials speak for themselves in the spaces they animate.

BERNARD TSCHUMI

CAFE DE LA VILLE

PARIS 1985–1987

"The norm contains the elements for explosion, deviance liberates them."
Bernard Tschumi.

Like the other *Folies* of Parc de la Villette, Cafe de la Ville is issued from the same matrix: a cube whose dimensions—10.80m for each spine—are relative to a base module 3.60m x 3.60m x 3.60m. This choice is not the result of chance. Rather, it derives from a social desire to share knowledge by delivering to the public a "disturbing" product of the imagination.

The subdivision into units of 3.60m allows for a large range of spatial modulations from which most of the architectural components are derived, from the structure, like the poles and beams, to the prefabricated panels, from the door to the window, etc. It also allows one to figure out typical surfaces, to evaluate volume, to assign a scale according to function. In a word, it is at the base of contemporary spatial organization; in fact, it is the explanation for the organization! This is why the basic module (3.60m x 3.60m x 3.60m) figures so well as the ideal cube, beside which all individual spatial practices seem arbitrary. It is the necessary condition to reach a higher perception of the project as a projection of the collective interest. Thus explained, the grid is the "rule of the game," a preamble to action; it is the norm at everyone's service; and everyone can enter into a game that becomes collective, social, urban. However, one risks falling into two faults: reproducing the rules of the game without playing the game, constructing a place that only reproduces the norm; or going off on a tangent and ignoring all rules, producing exclusive visions that are foreign to the social memory and therefore segregationist.

To these two approaches, indifference and rejection, Tschumi opposes civic values contained in the norm. Entirely based on the grid, Parc de la Villette has a community of objects—the *Folies*—all dressed in the same outfit of red enameled sheet-iron, supported by the same reinforced concrete armature made of stakes and beams of equal sections (.30 x .30), yet totally different from each other.

A strict application of the "rules of the game" engenders deviance that becomes itself a "Folie." And this time a human one. It reminds one of a crowd from which, occasionally, an acrobat, a fire eater, or a simple citizen elevated to the role of actor, steps out. Thirty-two times the eye will be thus captured by an anthropomorphic event, the profoundness of which has no limit: visually scanning the tiny Cafe de la Ville, we receive an echo of an excessiveness that humbles a little the arrogance of the large objects that haunt the park.

Client: *Établissement public du parc de la Villette.*
Location: *Parc de la Villette, 211 avenue Jean-Jaurès, Paris.*
Architect: *Bernard Tschumi.*
Company: *SMCE.*
Date of completion: *1987*
Floor area: *70 square meters (total area); 40 square meters (covered area).*

The recourse to a rigid orthogonal grid liberates Cafe de la Ville in space. In the background is the Grand Hall de la Villette.
Like the other Folies, the cafe rests on a primary structure composed of an assemblage of posts and beams of equal section, poured on the spot from adapted molds.
A red enamelled steel envelope covers every part of the reinforced concrete frame. It is designed to solve every interior or exterior corner, cantilever, or edge condition.

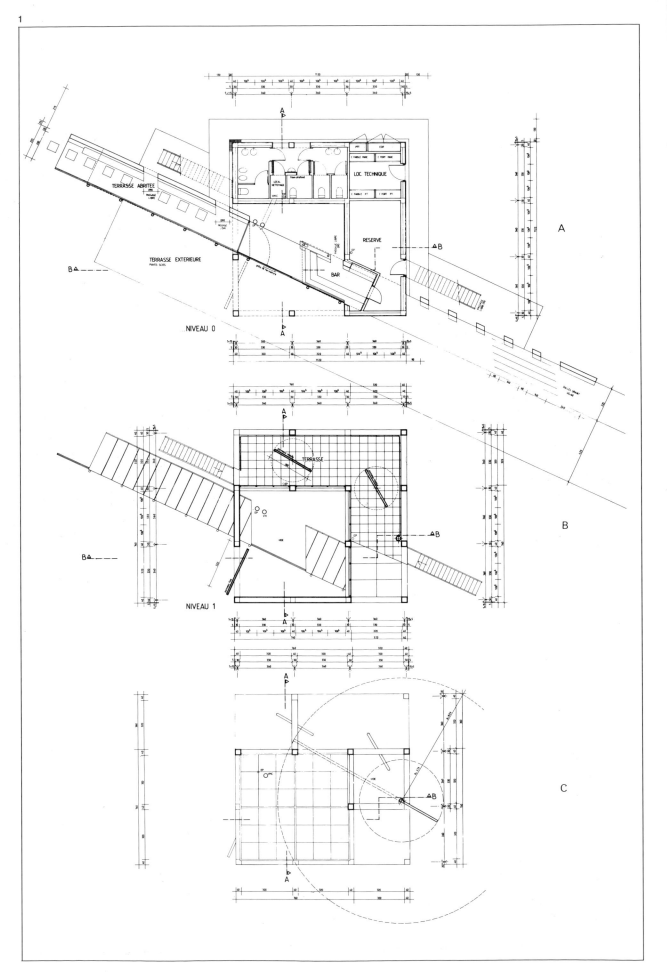

1. Plan of the levels of Cafe de la Ville.
A true open air cafe, the only parts of the
building that are fully enclosed are the
restrooms, the technical area, and the
special functions room. The dining area
is entirely open and allows the strollers
from the park great freedom of usage.
A. Plan of the ground floor.
B. Plan of the terrace.
C. Plan of the cover.

2. The "constructivist" architectures of
the 1920's are present in the free
shapes of Cafe de la Ville.

3. The alignment of the tables along the
granite wall seen from the central space
with, above, the balustrade from the
stairs leading to the terrace.

4. Perspective view of the cafe.
The granite wall sliding under the construction is reminiscent of familiar places
(patios, verandas) and, by its length,
counterbalances the vertical development of the cafe. This contradictory spatial perception introduces movement as
an integral part of the architecture. As a
result, the cafe cannot be fully ap-
prehended at a glance and reveals
surprising spatial depths dispropor-
tionate to its size.

2

3

4

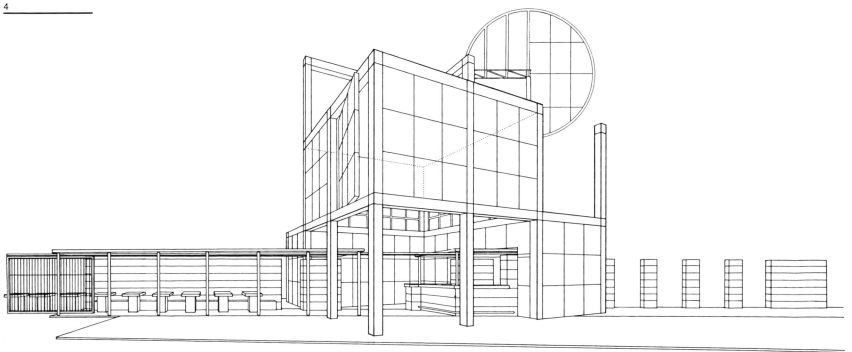

RICK MATHER

ZEN CENTRAL - ZEN W3

LONDON 1985–1987

Hampstead, Mayfair . . . in the shadows of these London neighborhoods are situated, respectively, Zen Central and Zen W3, pristine homages to Chinese cooking. The transparent facades of these two restaurants reveal the serene ordering of their internal structures. Light streams through the generous apertures in the roof, flooding these discreetly sophisticated places and soothingly diffusing throughout the space.

Within the sobriety of these two buildings, water—used as a decorative element—animates the material of the object that receives it. At Zen W3, water slides along the steps, ignoring the upward beckoning of the stair-

way. A shaft of sanded glass lying along the steps guides its course. At Zen Central water rests against the mirrors of the lateral partitions, as if suspended in the leaves of folded glass.

Tamed, almost palpable, the natural elements of water and light complete the decor and offer the visitor mutating images. Other, more tangible elements also contribute to the sobriety of the place: frail chrome structures underline the staircase, the counter of the bar, and even the backs and seats of the chairs; on the floor, the geometric rigor of the marble paving runs up against the scattered rod motif of the gray carpet.

The use of glass in a variety of ways allows for great clarity in the reading of the space, as well as for generous lighting. Utilized as another element of the decoration, the glass lends support to the creation of a certain tempo. As a mirror it captures light and diffuses it, doubling the volume. Opaque, sanded, or unpolished it functions sometimes as a bar counter or sometimes as a stair runner—at Zen Central, the name of the place is inscribed on the doors in opaque glass in the last room. In simple panes—invisible screens or indicators of an entrance—it opens the perspective, inviting light to wash over the depths of the spaces.

Client: *Lawrence Leung, Blaidwood.*
Location: *Zen Central, 20, 222 Queen Street Mayfair, London.*
Architects: *Rick Mather and Architects.*
Company: *Westbrooks.*
Date of completion: *June 1986.*
Floor area: *175 square meters.*

Client: *Lawrence Leung, Blaidwood.*
Location: *Zen W3, 83 Hampstead High Street, London W3.*
Architects: *Rick Mather and Architects.*
Company: *Westbrooks.*
Date of completion: *June 1987.*
Floor area: *308 square meters.*

1. At Zen Central, the round skylights dispense ample light into the area set back from the facade. Turned towards the room, the bar area is marked off by a change in the floor—marble paving— and by a difference in the height of the ceiling.

2. At Zen W3, a staircase whose balustrade, a tube of chromed steel, seems to float in space leads one to the second floor; a fine unpolished glass shaft, graduated to the steps, guides the course of the water.

1

2

1. Axonometric: large round skylights illuminate the back of the room. Set back from the main area in a curved panel on axis with the entrance is the bar.

2. In the evening, the clear facade reveals to the street the bright order of the interior spaces, the depth of which is opposed by the vertical rhythm of the metallic framing.

3. Detail of the bar: a chrome tubular structure supports the unpolished glass counter whose translucent clarity evokes water in movement.

2

1

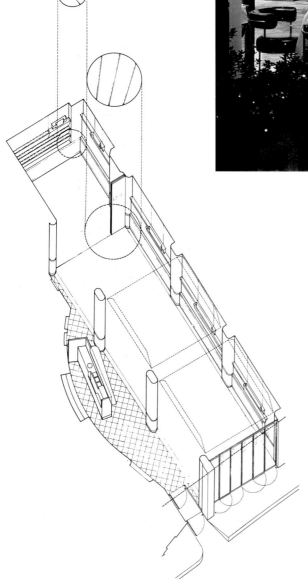

3

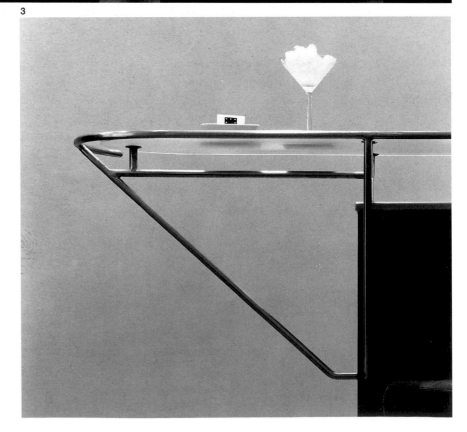

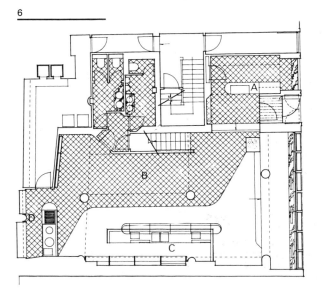

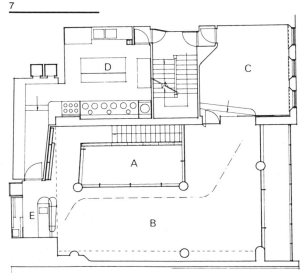

4. The second floor. The tables are disposed in an "L" around the central open space. The room is awash in light filtering through an entirely glassed facade and through a tilted skylight overhead.

5. On the ground floor some tables are set in a long narrow space as though on a terrace, set apart by a double-height skylight and the overhang of the ceiling.

6. Plan of the ground floor:
A. Entrance from street and coatroom.
B. Dining room.
C. Bar.
D. Pantry.

7. Plan of the second floor:
A. Empty area over the ground floor.
B. Main room.
C. Little room.
D. Kitchen.
E. Second floor pantry.

DAI REES

DIVA
GLASGOW 1986

Diva occupies the basement of a hotel in the Victorian city of Glasgow. One reaches it through an English courtyard, from the entrance vestibule of the hotel. To signal the entrance to the cafe, a rounded wall of glass paving blocks forms a small alcove in the vestibule; a little farther inside, a similar wall responds to it, shielding the bar, protecting the clients, and orienting newcomers towards the restaurant. Three steps and a change in floor finish (a protective rubber coating replaces the ceramic sand stone of the cafe) discreetly mark this shift in function within the same space. Disposed in a "U" around the bar, turned both towards the cafe and the restaurant, Diva uses a vocabulary that is particular to designers of the 1980's. The glass paving block partitions, the tiling of the floor, the perforated iron sheet, and the chrome create a universe that is greatly appreciated by the Glasgow "yuppies"—if one believes Rees who counted 195 people around the bar one spring evening.

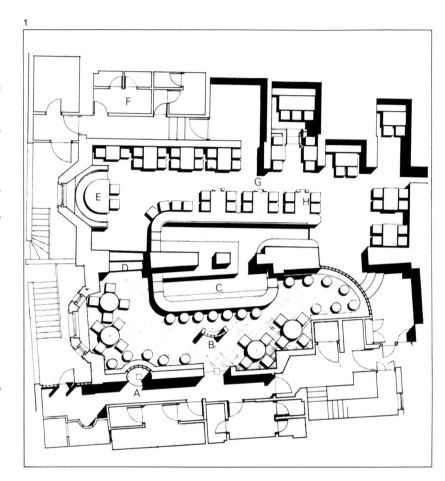

Client: *Spindent Ltd.*
Location: *Beacons Hotel, 9 Park Terrace, Glasgow.*
Architects: *Daï Rees Associates.*
Company: *Peter MacConnel.*
Date of completion: *October 1, 1986.*
Floor area: *185 square meters: 69 for the bar, 117 for the dining room.*
Cost: *Approximately 189,000 dollars.*

1. Plan:
A. Entrance hall of the hotel.
B. Glass-tiled wall screening the bar.
C. Bar.
D. Three steps separating the cafe from the restaurant.
E. Alcove wall-sofas.
F. Restrooms.
G. Restaurant.
H. High tables adjoining the restaurant's bar.

2. 3. 4. 5. In the city of Glasgow, the light filtering out of the blue blinds is the only clue to Diva. Nothing in the streets prepares one for the clean atmosphere within, where steel, glass, and earthenware coolly mix in a variety of ways.

2

3

4

5

JIRICNA/KERR ASSOCIATES

JOE'S CAFE
LONDON 1986

A glass door sunk in a large glass bay opens on the main room of the cafe: the steel chrome tubes of the rounded bar, the cutout of the white ceiling above the dark counter, and the longitudinal lines drawn by the jointing of the tiles accentuate the perspective.

At the far end of the counter is a room whose contours form a truncated triangle; four pillars belonging to the original structure give rhythm to the long axis of this space. Steel cables connect the top part of each pillar, covered in black granito, to a railing treated like a netting. This minimal protection in the alignment of the pillars also marks a shift in levels (noticeably equal to the height of a table) which carves two rooms within one space.

The white ceiling saturated with halogen lamps seems to float, while on the walls the irregular sinews of the plaster soften the initial geometry of the place and conceal the piping. The minimal use of color, the lighting, and even the use of certain materials like metal or granite create a decoration that is typical of the high tech style of posh neighborhoods.

1 _____

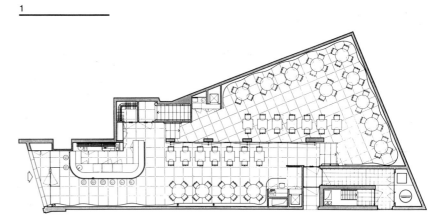

Client: *Joseph Ltd.*
Location: *126 Draycott Avenue, London SW3.*
Architects: *Jiricna/Kerr Associates.*
Company: *P. M. Construction Ltd.*
Structures: *Price & Myers.*
Mechanics and electricity: *Yates Associates.*
Carpentry: *Matt Marchbank.*
Doors: *Syspal Ltd.*
Opening date: *February 1986.*
Floor area: *Ground floor, 170.5 square meters; basement, 85.2 square meters.*
Cost: *Approximately 630,000 dollars.*

1. 2. 3. Unaffected by the shift in levels, a plaster wainscot undulates along the wall, in irregular waves, concealing the piping.
Above the bar and set back from a black soffit, the ceiling, punctuated by halogen spots, seems to float in space. The same back granito finish covers the floor and the pillars, which are connected to a railing by steel cables.

DENIS SANTACHIARA

L'AQUYLONE
REGGIO EMILIA 1986

"My intention is to extend the concept of a fixed decor to an animated one, the theatre of immaterial performances."
Denis Santachiara.

As opposed to domestic spaces, public spaces engage contradictory interests, assembling individuals who are *a priori* strangers. It is a space not only for the disparate, but also for cultural and commercial exchange. Languages are made and unmade in the confusion of lifestyles. Communication is therefore constantly in question, not just as the basis for all convivial behavior, but also, and this is an important paradox, as the cornerstone of the marketing system in which we live.

In his architecture, Santachiara echoes this disturbing duality, which he hopes to transcend, by introducing sensationalism through advanced techniques of sound and image. Caught in a cinematographic web, the public must, in principle, renounce all passive or noncommunicative behavior in order to evolve towards an "interactive" state, which generates surprising complicities. The finality of the project will then no longer be the architecture itself, but rather what it authorizes thanks to its formal apparatus. An aesthetic of emotions results, which draws its vocabulary from an enigmatic electronic naturalism. Conceived, as it is, for an eccentric public, fond of refined fast-food, Aquylone (literally, "the kite")

is a good example of Santachiara's endeavor. A painstaking staging of the under spaces gives them each their own status. One could cite here as examples the ventilated sofa and the little television in the "waiting room," the optic fibres encrusted in the resin floor boards of the clearing area, the vibrations of an imaginary subway in the "salon of disenchanted youth," and the simulated storm in the garden full of real and plastic plants of the intimate salon.
In this succession of unexpected and strange events, the customer is constantly solicited. He is given no rest, and according to the rules of fast-food, time goes by very quickly. The architecture has communicated its image.

Client: *"Aguylone" Society.*
Location: *8 Via Caggiati, Reggio Emilia.*
Architect: *Denis Santachiara.*
Collaborator: *Vincenzo Pellegrini, Architect.*
Date of completion: *June 1986*
Floor area: *240 square meters.*
Cost: *Approximately 118,000 dollars; 492 dollars per square foot.*

A metallic torch spits out an electric flame and signals the entrance to the fast-food restaurant. In this space animated by immaterial sensations, the client travels from surprise to surprise before tasting the delicious specialties of Reggio Emilia. We see in the foreground the sofa of the "waiting room" with, behind the brushed steel screen (mounted on wheels), the "salon of disenchanted youth." Optic fibers have been encrusted in the resin floor to orient the visitor.

1. The "salon of disenchanted youth" with the restaurant's menu hanging on the wall. Buried in the floor, a sound mechanism simulating a subway goes off regularly, causing the room to vibrate. The sounds of a large metropolis have come to haunt a space with no history in this provincial Italian town.

2. The room with the round tables with fake electric furnaces placed in the middle. Behind the scene in the photograph, two glassed doors open on an electronic garden overflowing with real and plastic plants where, at regular intervals, a violent storm breaks that lasts six minutes. After this artificial tempest, the light rises in a crescendo and birds start to sing. In the back, another brushed steel screen conceals the exit.

3. The sofa in the "waiting room" is animated by a ventilation mechanism that imitates the irregular and continuous blowing of wind. At its feet, one discovers a tiny television encrusted in the floor and optic fibers with a trailing of luminous specks. The programs for these images and effects are constantly changed.

4. General axonometric for the fast-food restaurant. This shows the "U" shaped design and, in gray, the path of the optic fibers:
A. Entrance.
B. Salon of disenchanted youth.
C. Room with circular tables.
D. The electronic garden.
E. Exit.

5. Sketch of a triangular table with incorporated lighting (as seen in the "salon of disenchanted youth"). The decor and the furniture were entirely conceived by Denis Santachiara.

6. Sketch for the brushed steel screen on wheels, with the hooks that serve as coat hangers.

1

2

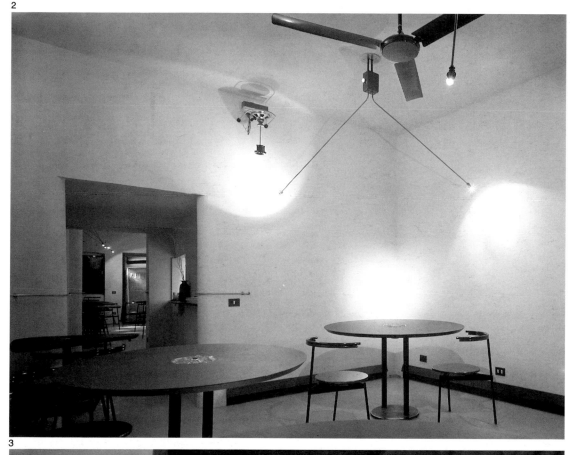

3

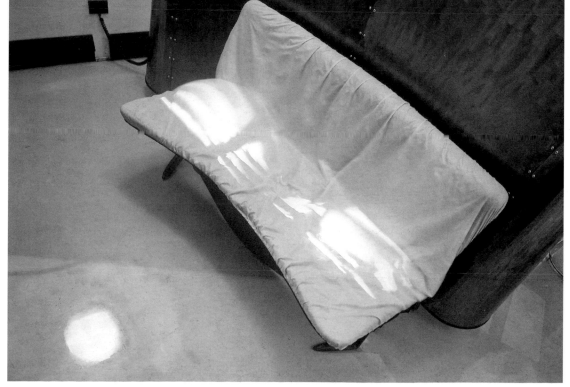

4

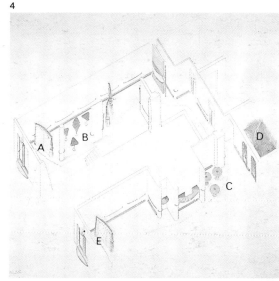

5

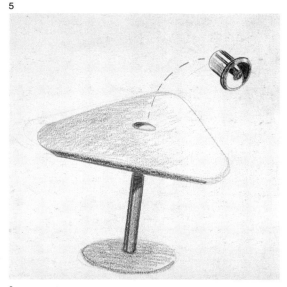

6

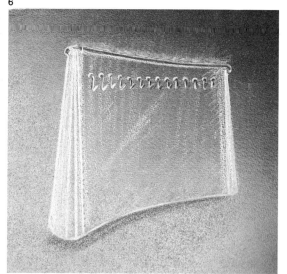

MULTIMEDIA "FACTORIES OF PLEASURE"

"To be good, a cafe must be black as night, warm as hell, and soft as love . . ."
Bakounine, quoted by Giorgio Conti.

The persistence of unemployment, an increasingly fugitive sense of identity linked to accelerated changes in production, an exacerbated individuality, and loss of older community values are the backdrops of the 1980's. This context of crisis, where all social reason seems absent, does not have only negative results. It also engenders a general behavior that is more attentive to novelty. This could explain the good fortune that the new "temples of leisure," which are flourishing on the banks of the Romagne, know today. Built on a program that confers a productive value on games and their byproducts, these spaces, which are entirely equipped with computers, are above all tools at the service of individual creativity: they can be appropriated, adapted, transformed to meet the needs of the moment. Leisure as "pure activity" has outstripped leisure as "pure consumption." Of the projects presented, the most significant are perhaps Barcellona at Rimini and Baia Imperiale at Gabicce Monte. The first was conceived expressly by creative people for creative people. Purposely droll, the entrance is ritualized by a brief initiation: the instructions for usage change according to the user. Then, starting from recognized clues—the billiards room, the bowling room, the ballroom—the visitor familiarizes himself with the space and with the unusual places: the tunnel library, the video infrastructure, the ecological bar. Imbued with all these multimedia visions, he passes into action, improvises his performance, programs his encounters, and sells his productions.
The Roman ostentation of Baia Imperiale echoes this aim to be avant-garde: its scenery was even built at Cinecitta. The Grand Temple, Temple of Venus, the Lions Bar, and the Imperial Swimming Pool resonate with the highest technological sophistication: laser beams, cosmic bombings, strobe lights. This grand architectural movie set, elevated by hords of visitors to the rank of monument, marks the birth of the big multimedia "factories of pleasure." Whether this event, planned to cover a whole region, will be in the tradition of the famous Cafe Pedrocchi of Padua, precursor of a society of the third type, or, on the contrary, a sublime remake in the lively tradition of profit making, only time will tell.

Client: "Bowling" Society, S.R.L.
Location: Barcellona, 119 viale Vespucci, Rimini.
Architect: Studio Ciavatti.
Opening date: December 1986.
Floor area: 1,000 square meters.

Client: "Nuova Baia degli Angeli" Society.
Location: Baia Imperiale, Gabicce Monte, Pesaro.
Architect: Studio Tausani-Ferrini and Associates.
Opening date: January 1985.
Floor area: 4,000 square meters.

Iconography: Gian Guido Palumbo, Architect.
Bibliography: Georgio Conti, architect and professor in the Department of Urbanism at the Venice Architecture Institute.

Baia Imperiale (Gabicce Monte): restaurant in the 1960's, discotheque in the 1970's, this place, laid out like the spread of a bird's wings, was redone in 1985. The decor, executed in Rome at the studios of Cinecitta, evokes the pomp of antique Rome and consecrates the birth of new forms of communication at the service of mass tourism.
Barcellona (Rimini): after the Festival "Tendencias '85," organized in Barcelona on the theme of the creativity of youth, this old garage, turned into a bowling alley in 1980, became a laboratory of active leisure in 1986 where relaxation, information, and work are combined.

Baia Imperiale

1. The imperial entrance in the early morning: the neoclassical language encloses highly sophisticated technology.

2. The Temple of Venus, set up as an incandescent dance floor where artificial suns periodically set.

3. The Lion Bar facing the Temple of Venus.
The satyr bar, the swimming pool, and the amphitheater are other spatial elements of Baia, which can hold 1,500 people.

Barcellona

4. The two entrances to Barcellona.

5. The billiards room.

6. The ecological bar with a video corner in the back.
The establishment also has a "tunnel-library" with avant-garde periodicals, instantaneous exposition spaces, a bowling alley, etc. It can welcome 500 people.

Some other establishments of the "third type."

7. Bandiera Gialla (Rimini) : the "baby-disco" dance floor, sponsored by Benetton for "hip" children.

8. Ku (Riccione): the neo-Roman terrace of a large villa transformed into a Temple of Transgression.

9. Lele Marlène (Misano Adriatico): set up for a season in an old car track, this travelling establishment, symbolically split by a wall, was meant as a homage to Berlin.

LA PACE
TURIN 1984

In the restoration world, brick is often associated with wood, and together they compose the so called "rustic style" characteristic of innumerable pizzeria chains. But one can also reverse the cliché of brick to create less banal, quite unique atmospheres. Accordingly, the architects of Invenzione chose a subtle alliance of materials to destroy all stereotypes and give back to brick its nobility. The reciprocities created by the sandstone, the marble, or even the brass and the glass affect the fixed elements of the decor, like the wall facing and the floor finish as well as certain elements of the furniture.

The fine Siennese columns of green and white marble posed along the spines of the bays reveal the textures of the brick and the irregular joints, and receive in exchange a more natural setting, safe from all sophisticated interpretation. The floor, in crushed sandstone and marble, answers, in apparent disorder, the willfully scrambled grid of the brickwork and little columns. This play of connections introduces into the interiors an atmosphere of gravity defying suspension. The "immaterial" presence of fine glass partitions accentuates this feeling of detachment from the usual static and formal givens. The pigmentation of the floor, the melting of the wall facings, and the reflections of the glasswork give the ensemble an expressive coherence that is a backdrop for isolated events, which are necessary for the functioning of the place. Thus, the dessert tray, formed of layered circular glass slivers, symmetrically doubled by many mirrors, evokes an independent architectural figure, almost insinuating by reflection the presence of imaginary windows in the ceiling. An anchoring to conventional style becomes impossible thanks to the almost live presence of the Murano glass and brass lamps. These lamps—baptized "soldiers" by their creators—seem to be mounting guard against all intrusion of cliché. Under their impassive eye other actors of unknown reference, such as the suspended umbrella holder, the motifs drawn in the floor, or the colored glass squares encrusted in the glass partitions, find their exact places. Rigor and freedom are thus associated to create a very personalized and original space that the presence of familiar materials makes accessible to a family clientele well acquainted with the fine cooking of La Pace.

Client: *Mr. and Mrs. Cellini.*
Location: *Via Bernardino Galliari 22, Turin.*
Architect: *Invenzione.*
Company: *Bosco.*
Date of completion: *1984.*
Floor area: *200 square meters.*
Cost: *Approximately 137,000 dollars; 685 dollars per square meter.*

The fixing up of the restaurant La Pace demanded complex demolition and reconstruction. The conservation of masonry and structures that turned out to be necessary has not been concealed. This false clumsiness, visible in the assemblage of the bricks, introduces a surprising animation in the walls.
In spite of it's "bad reputation," brick remains one of the noble materials of architecture. Its omnipresence does not preclude the usage of very dissimilar accompanying materials, for example the little marble columns and the crushed sandstone and marble floor.
The Sol-Dato lamps (literally: "soldier") advancing over the Thonet tables and chairs have a brass structure with a colored Murano glass shade.

1. *Lateral view of the entrance hall with the dessert rack.*
The purposely scrambled grid of the bricks and little columns converse with the apparent disorder of the crushed sandstone and marble floor. This project, executed in record time (45 days) required the daily presence of the architects and specialized artisans. This allowed for improvisation and an absolute mastery of the project in the space.

2. *Elevation and color study of the walls and the integrated furniture that separate the dining room and the kitchen, across from the entrance.*

3. *Elevation and color study of a partition in plaster squares that closes one of the blind ends of the establishment.*

4. *Plan of the restaurant: the big white space is the kitchen, and in the entrance hall, the white element is the dessert rack.*

5. *Plan of the light sources.*

1

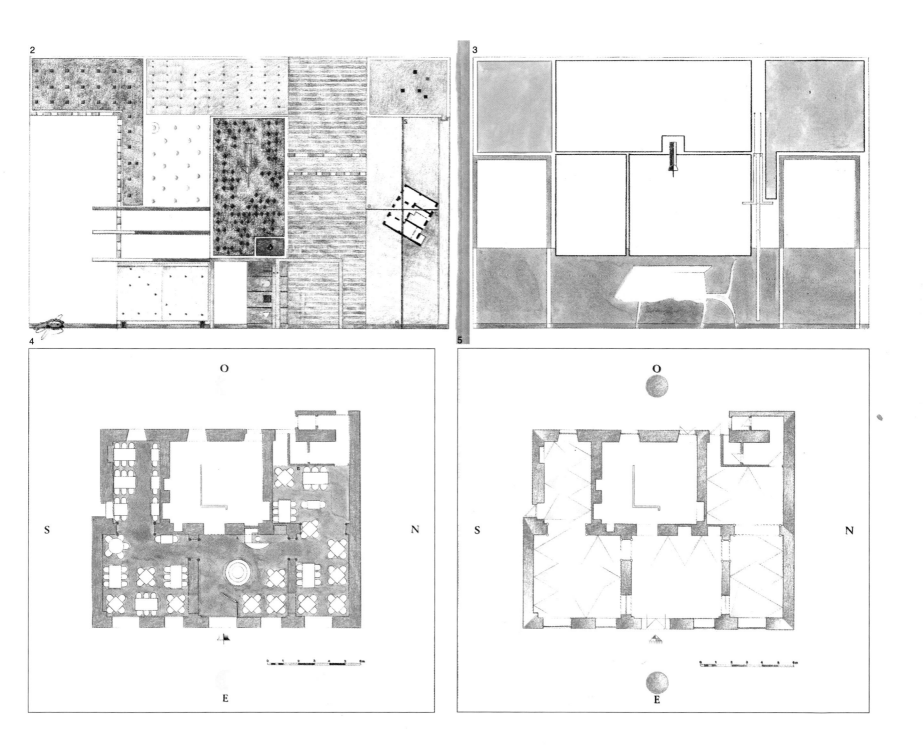

TADAO ANDO

MON PETIT CHOU
KYOTO 1985

"Because I am Japanese, I was able to cultivate a sense of beauty in simplicity, and I hope, in using the modern material of concrete and its purified wall, to attain a Japanese sense of space."
Tadao Ando.

In this residential neighborhood of Kyoto, Mon Petit Chou is a parallelepiped half-buried, covered by an arc formed by a sixth of a circle. A wall in the shape of a quarter circle meets this "box" at its extremity. The concise and transparent envelope of this *cake house* presents a retail counter in the entrance space to which a large room with tables set some steps up responds.

The architecture bends to the geometric rigor of Tadao Ando: an absolute geometry, made up only of squares and circles that despise ornament. It draws its strength and its autonomy from the material that gives it shape: "When concrete adheres to the aesthetic image that I have conceived, the surface of the wall joins, through abstraction, nothingness and approaches the limit of space."
Inside the building the eye slides over wood steps, then over the brutal surfaces of the concrete walls whose flat gray surfaces fade away little by little; what remains is the perception of a space surrounded and made hierarchical by a play of different levels. In this constructed "emptiness," the path of the arc and the curve of the wall make the space dynamic and exaggerate the longitudinal axis of the building. This suggested movement is carried on along the arched partition on both floors.
At the end of this passage, a secret courtyard covered in greens seems to turn toward the sky; it marks the real limit of the space, beyond the bay window through which light streams. In the sobriety of this architecture, the concrete, raw and smooth, gives its own tone to the space; the shapes and the materials are subdued, as if the place existed by the sheer rigor of the geometry.

Location: *Kyoto.*
Architect: *Tadao Ando.*
Furniture design: *Shiro Kuramata.*
Date of completion: *April 1985.*
Floor area: *322.85 square meters.*

View from the ground floor mezzanine looking over the dining room located in the basement that looks out on the inclined green space. The absence of window frames allows for the raw encounter of the materials: concrete, parquet, and glass.

Bar Lucchino.

1. Axonometric.

2. A sliver of light runs along the beam over the bar; the dimensions of the beam are closer to those of a ceiling than to an isolated element of the structure.

3. The wall, covered in aluminum particles, fades away, leaving only the curved lines of the partition (echoed in the light points in the false ceiling) and the shimmer of the material.

1

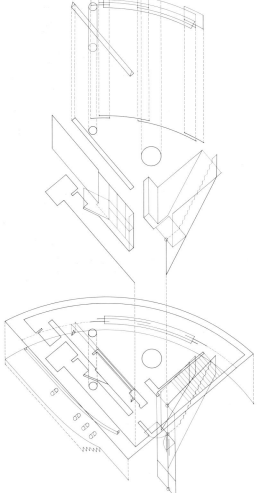

2

3

Cafe Oxy.

4. Here, the lighting under the floor and the choice of the materials (transparent resin flagstones and stainless steel joints) give light the leading role. The table in the foreground does not destroy the effect of the freely diffused light; its shape and colors establish a necessary counterpoint and disrupts the luminous grid on the floor.

PHILIPPE STARCK

MANIN
TOKYO 1986

"This project expresses the reasons that push me to design public spaces—to create the violence and drama that are inconceivable in a private space." Philippe Starck.

Buried in the bowels of a building in Tokyo, the restaurant Manin is like a strange theatre, closed in on itself. Within the project, each element has its own role and participates in the composition of the drama. The curtain rises on a fragile aluminum bridge: delicate, unstable, trembling at the lightest passage, it stretches over the huge emptiness down to the bar. Suddenly, a monumental staircase rushes to the bottom of a tilted partition covered in red velvet. From the top of the stairs, newcomers appear like actors emerging from an imaginary backstage. From the bar, the dining room and the large back wall appear to be from another scene.

Sheltered from the drama, beams and pillars in black granite give rhythm to the depth of the room. They complete the staging of a game between emptiness and preciousness: "All my spaces are conceived like opera scenery," declares Philippe Starck, and one has to deserve the privilege of access to this performance. Emotion has no price.

1 _____

Client: *Person's Co Ltd.*
Location: *2-22-12 Jingumae, Shibuya-ku, Tokyo.*
Architect: *Philippe Starck.*
Company: *Casatec Limited.*
Opening date: *November 1986.*
Floor area: *220 square meters.*

In this luxurious setting (red velvet padding and blond mahogany veneer) entirely conceived in Paris, thanks to a fax machine, the earthquake-proof structure plated in black granite gives rhythm to the backdrop.

2

3

4

5

SHIN TAKAMATSU

DANCE HALL
NAGOYA 1985

"One must have faith in the material, for its strength is the exact measure of the depth of criticism."
Shin Takamatsu

There are no signs on this place. Only two rusty pillars mark the entrance: they circle the void and make the darkness attractive. A massive door with a gray handle, still warm from the last hand, defends the vestibule; blue cracks, leaning, all in one direction, disrupt the perspective and the geometry of this dark hallway. At the back, a silver door opens on a staggering spectacle: over 2,000 lamps caught under the glass tiles and the steel grill of the floor, waiting for the signal from the music. Suddenly, multicolored beams shoot in every direction. Projectors placed between the beams combine their strobe-light effects with the movement of the dancers. Spacial perception teeters, and the steel structure, swept by laser beams, seems to turn to liquid.

1

Client: *IDX Co Ltd.*
Location: *Nagoya-Aichi Prefecture.*
Architect: *Shin Takamatsu.*
Date of completion: *September 1985.*
Floor area: *375 square meters.*

1.2. The ambiguous, almost prison-like space of the access corridor is played against the vast, but equally disturbing, space of the dance floor. Responding to the music, the bodies of the dancers, glorified by the lighting arrangement, seem to break apart. Along the metallic walls, the aligned projectors look like bolts in the beams.

1. The cafe with chairs designed by the French designer Philippe Starck, the overhang of the interior facade, and the restaurant with the tables, lighting, and lighting fixtures designed by the Opera Design group.

2. The entrance to the theatre, with its zinc door.

3. Giant cutlery and plates drawn on the floor of the restaurant.

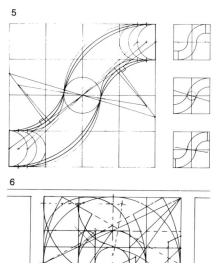

4. The entirely reconstructed false facade of Cafe de Unie. On the right is a glimpse of the neutral shaft where the technical elements are concentrated and, overhead, the setback facade of the offices.

In 1925, J. P. P. Oud wrote of his cafe: "The upper right corner is vermillion red, the left side is canary yellow; the semicylinders over the light sign are gray, as are the two dark bands that delimit the facade; the top cylinder is yellow. The lower frames are ultramarine blue [while] the little windows above them are gray and white with black corners. The capital letters in the sign are white on a blue background . . . the sign on top has gray capitals on black, with yellow lanterns . . . the flat wall is white." (Cited by the Opera Design group).

5. 6. 7. Graphic studies for the signs.

EDUARDO SOUTO DE MOURA

CAFE DU MARCHÉ
BRAGA 1984

This cafe is ideally located on the crest of a slight knoll that is crossed by the ochre stone wall of the municipal market, also designed by Souto de Moura. Its architecture unfolds in a surprising succession of static effects, which seem to constantly threaten its equilibrium. The curved wall of quarry stone from an old grain depot and a fine glass partition, punctuated by painted steel frames, seem to single-handedly support an imposing slab of white cement. This slab is partially echoed by another vertical one, which is an "L" shape resting on a practically invisible bent metallic element. This opposition of materials and radical (but deceptive) inversion of their functions gives a feeling of strength and fragility, a reminder of the conflict between the new and the old.

This building, a catalyst for the tensions in the site, stands out sharply in a landscape of decrepit stone houses that alternate with modern buildings. It signals from afar, like the old village churches, the presence of the market. Unfortunately, the cafe remains unfinished and probably never will be completed. The new municipality passed a decree for its demolition.

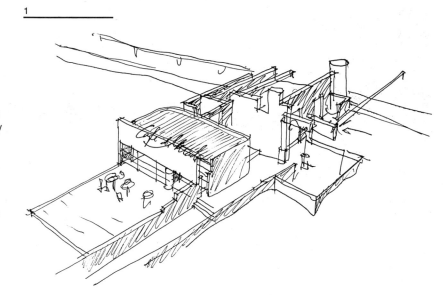

1

Client: *Braga Municipality.*
Location: *Municipal market of Braga.*
Architect: *Eduardo Souto de Moura.*
Collaborators: *Joao Mesquita, Joao Carreira.*
Date of completion: *1984.*
Floor area: *105 square meters.*

1. Sketch for Cafe du Marché.
2. View of the cafe from the stone stairway.
3. The flagstone and the vertical slab become almost one architectural element. The thin glass partition is mounted on metallic frames.
4. The vertical plane over the crumbling stone constructions crystallizes the tensions of the site.
5. The unstable equilibrium of the cafe is created by the succession of materials: the curved quarry stone wall, the flagstone, the vertical white cement plane, the glass panes, and the metal pilar. An old stone house turns its back on the more recent constructions. Invaded by weeds, the cafe awaits demolition, all mediation between the old and the new seems impossible.

KARL AND MAX DÜDLER

CAFE-BAR
FRANKFURT 1986

The two windows, located symmetrically on either side of the opaque entrance to this place, open the cafe and the bar directly onto the street. This old bakery was entirely stripped but recovered a mysterious, dramatic tonality thanks to the mirrors the architects placed on the back wall, directly on axis with the windows. The spaces, clearly defined by the opposition of the interior facades, are suddenly multiplied and simulate two perfectly aligned streets to infinity. This recourse to a purified rationalism gives the space a strange sobriety in which a dry functionalism smoothly encounters its appropriate form. This perfect osmosis between form and content sometimes leads to solutions that go against conventions but that are necessary for the inner logic of the space. Thus, the bold grouping of the restrooms and the service areas on the axis of the two facades separating the cafe and the bar is a concession to practicality and a strong point of the architectural composition. In the same way, the three openings that cross this middle line are cut like doors to a building and are equidistant from each other. They frame the main visual axis perfectly, although they should have upset it.

The little windows punctuating the top part of the two facades also respond equally to two imperatives: to create perspective and to serve at the same time as a support for the lighting.

Between the physical limitations of the old bakery and the artificial limitations of the new cafe-bar, no confusion is possible. Past and present preserve their singular qualities and make manifest their autonomy. Thus, two levels of perception act simultaneously: the first in relation to the real limitations of the space, the wall, and the ceiling; the second in relation to the illusion of space reflected in the mirrors.

Without any flourish and with only the cooperation of the right angle, the black and white decor theatricalizes and shelters (especially at the start of inclement weather) the furtive encounters of the city.

Client: *Mrs. Hildebrandt.*
Location: *14 Schweizerstrasse, Frankfurt.*
Architects: *Karl and Max Düdler.*
Opening date: *1986.*
Floor area: *110 square meters.*
Cost of construction: *Approximately 154,000 dollars; 1,400 dollars per square meter.*

Behind its two great windows, surmounted by a reflective band in black lacquered wood, Cafe-Bar evokes a fragment of the city built on immovable architectural principles. On the back wall, on axis with these two windows, two mirrors extend the perspective and simulate two parallel streets running on eternally. The black and white decor, stripped of all formal sophistication, replaces, in its cold immobility, the citizen-consumer at the center of the spectacle.

1

2

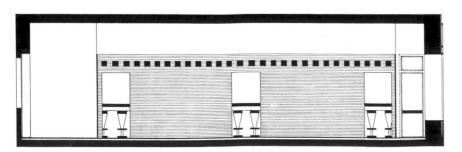 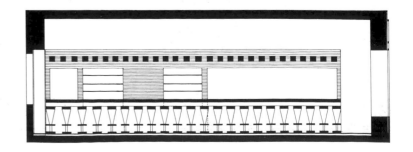

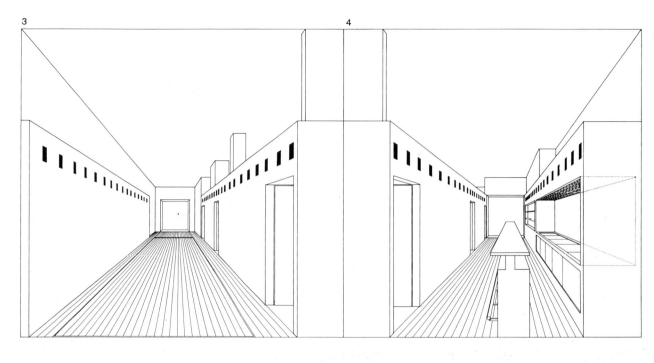

3

4

1. In this old bakery, two levels of perception are simultaneously at work: the first is in relation to the physical limits of the space; the second to the illusion of space reflected in the two mirrors and in the brilliance of the interior facade of black lacquered wood. The architects have left a considerable space between the new decor and the existing ceiling with its moldings and stucco motifs.

2. Crosscut of the cafe (left) with the three cuts that lead to the bar. Crosscut of the bar (right): the height of the interior facades is regulated by the height of the windows. The long reflective band on the exterior indicates the actual height of the place.

3. Perspective view of the cafe.

4. Perspective view of the bar.
Each little window hides a light bulb as well as defines the perspective.

5. General plan of Cafe-Bar: the restrooms and service areas have been cleverly grouped on axis with the entrance door.
A. Entrance.
B. Bar.
C. Cafe.
D. Restrooms and service areas.
E. Corridors.

5

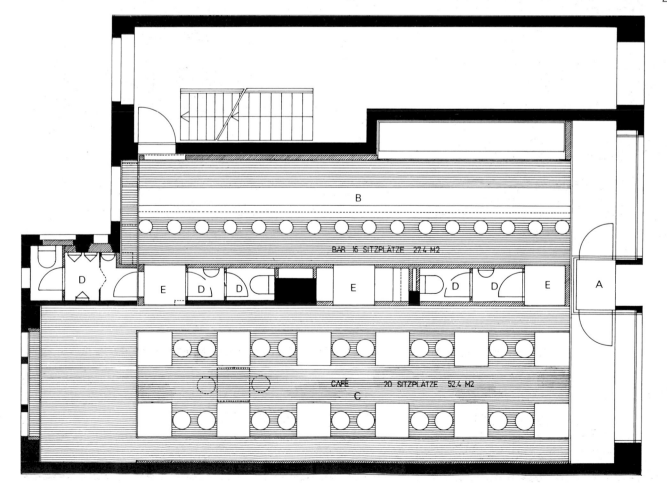

BAR 16 SITZPLÄTZE 27.4 M2

CAFÉ 20 SITZPLÄTZE 52.4 M2

ARNOLD AND VRENDLI AMSLER

CAFE SCHURTER
ZURICH 1984

Cafe Schurter is installed in a medieval building in central Zurich that forms the angle of two perpendicular streets. Although this is a privileged location, it does have some inconveniences. As the cafe was an intervention in an historically protected site, all modifications to the facade had to conform to a strict code, which left the architects very little freedom of creation.

This is the price one must pay in order to safekeep both a patrimony and a collective memory. But for Arnold and Vrendli Amsler, these measures became arbitrary, because they are applied indiscriminately to all old buildings, regardless of their architectural value. Worse than that, they claim, the measures are inoperative because badly conceived. Apparently, the rules to preserve architecture only apply to the upper levels of the buildings; the ground floors are not as tightly controlled. Under commercial pressure, supporting walls have been eliminated, doors have

been widened and a "display window" mentality has completely upset the original spatial organization of protected sites. This split between the street level and the upper floors, between the urban function and the restricting function, underlines the incoherence of the policies of historic preservation.

This is why, in Cafe Schurter, the architects wished to re-establish a link between the ground floor and the other floors. The cornice that ran along the ground floor has been simplified, allowing the building to find a verticality and coherence it was lacking.

This prudent but thoughtful intervention is maintained inside the cafe. Without modifying the disposition of the supporting walls, the architects used basic geometric figures to re-organize the space: the cylinder services the cafe and the candy store, and the three cubes are reflected on the floor by the design of three squares that defines the counter

area. This reasonable geometry gives the irregular spaces of the cafe a calculated status without freezing the space. The oblique positioning of the counter creates a dynamic that accentuates the depth of the place. In the same way, the mirrors inserted in the grillwork separating the candy store and the cafe dilate the space laterally, canceling the "corridor" effect. These contrasts in volume allow for a maximum use of the area and a *trompe-l'œil* effect that pushes back the physical limits of the cafe.

A work of limitations, a space within a space, Cafe Schurter is the result of an interpretation of constraints, using them to generate ideas. It is a very urban response to the false mimicry suggested by the authorities. Having to choose between respect for tradition and novelty in architecture, Arnold and Vrendli Amsler chose the former because, after all, a cafe belongs to everyone, and everyone can enjoy Cafe Schurter.

Client: *Mrs. Michel.*
Location: *Niederdorfstrasse, Central, Zurich.*
Architects: *Arnold and Vrendli Amsler.*
Construction began: *May 1984.*
Duration of construction: *6 months.*
Floor area: *80 square meters.*

View of the entrance and cafe from the candy shop: closed on the side of the shop, open on that of the cafe, the glass cylinder introduces a doubled circular movement that broadens the visual field but is limited by the long, narrow configuration of the premises. The two entrances are off-center, allowing one to appreciate the space diagonally, making it seem both larger and more surprising.

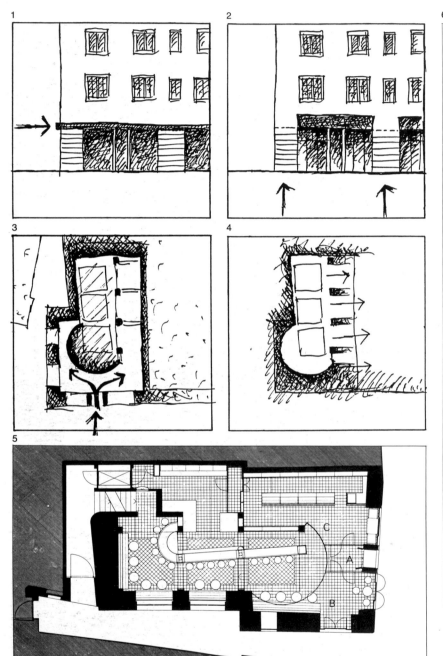

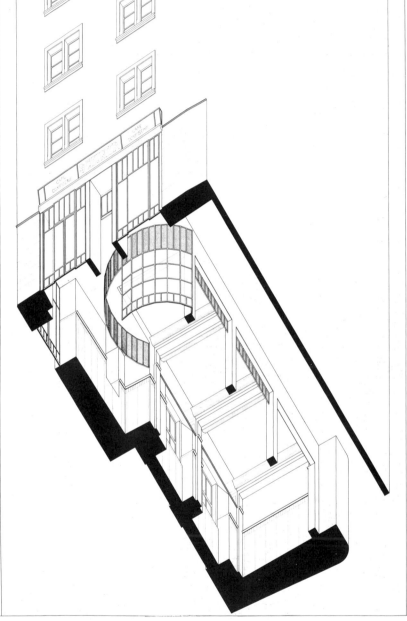

1. Study sketch of the exterior facade before the architects' intervention; the arrow indicates the demarcation line between the ground floor, given to commerce, and the other floors, which are protected by strict urban regulations.

2. Study sketch of the exterior facade: the line arbitrarily separating the ground floor from the others disappears and the building recovers its old coherence in which the base and floors participate in the same composition.

3. The existing spatial constraints are less an obstacle for the project than a departure point; the cylinder and the three cubes structure the space and give the irregular areas a calculated status.

4. The placement of each function presupposes a spatial hierarchy: the arrows indicate where the service areas will be.

5. Plan of Cafe Schurter:
A. The entrance screen.
B. The cafe.
C. The candy store.
The oblique positioning of the counter picks up the diagonal perception of the space suggested by the lateral entrances and makes it even more dynamic. Not visible in the picture, the mirrors inserted in the grillwork separating the cafe and the candy store expand the space widthwise, counteracting the "corridor" effect.

6. The underside of Cafe Schurter: axonometric traced on the bottom.

7. The curve at the end of the counter echoes the curve of the cylinder. Every corner of the cafe is used, and the sobriety of the decor gives free reign to a discreet friendliness.

8. The entrance to the cafe, with the candy store behind the counter. The first of the three cubes that structure the volume of the cafe is drawn on the tiles.

FROM THE BAR . . .

The bar is open!
As a key figure in the place, the bar must immediately catch the eye. It must also draw the visitor in from the entrance, maybe even from the street. It is in itself a place of consumption, and all possible feelings of loneliness must be banished from it. The consumers—potential regulars, members of a more or less closed inner circle—must be able to intervene in the constant hustle and bustle of movements and conversations, they must be able to participate in the game of seduction.

But this place for meeting and congeniality also has functional needs and components. Whether concealed or in plain sight, these elements are in any case essential to the well-being of the client. A screen protects the standard items—a dishwasher, refrigerated stocks, etc. But the objects of desire—bottles, glasses, or coffee machines—are exposed and become a part of the designer's composition. As to the counter of the bar, a custom-made item, it often participates in some spatial stage setting, reinforced by sophisticated lighting and unexpected materials.

Rather than presiding over the space, as in a cafe or bar, the bar in a restaurant is conceived of more as a waiting place—a purgatory to cross before attaining the paradise of the dining room. The shape of the bar in this case is less congenial: its main function is to direct the client towards the tables.

ZEN

In London, the bar of the restaurant Zen Central is set back from the dining room, turning its back to it. A tubular, steel chrome structure connects the frosted glass sheet to the shiny surfaces of the block of the bar; the projection of the countertop allows one to sit at it.

MANIN

At the Manin restaurant in Tokyo, a "decompression" landing between the little footbridge and the final descent towards the dining room serves as a bar. In lieu of a counter, a slab of blue glass shimmers like a jewel under the light of the spots in the floor. The wall behind it makes up the sideboard where all the service takes place.

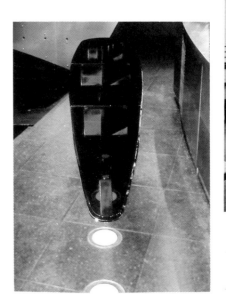

KGB * (Spain)

The counter at KGB bar in Barcelona is conceived as an autonomous piece of furniture. A mobile wagon mounted on wheels, its illuminated partition walls hint at the silhouettes of the bottles stocked under a metallic looking countertop.

REISS BAR (Austria)

The constraining dimensions of the Reiss Bar in Vienna led the architects to put in a "U" shaped counter in the central position. Picking up in a controlled manner the architects' theme of a fault, the angles of the counter are emptied out and protected by rounded glass. Above it, two suspended "beams" hold the glasses.

TOSCANA * (U.S.A.)

The luxurious bar of Toscana restaurant in New York is conceived as a curved partition in precious wood. On the lower part, the alternating of light and dark wood accentuates the curve, which is repeated above the marble counter in a band of pear tree wood. In the back, ignoring this play of curves, the bottles are aligned in rectangular shelves connected to the clearing space by chromed steel tubes.

BUFFET DE LA GARE * (France)

The bar of Buffet de la Gare in Plourin-Plougonven offers an example of symmetrical composition. The central linear motif echoes the vertical lines of the metallic squared irons supporting the shelving spaces above the counter.

CAFE OXY

By adopting a geometric solution, Oxy pushes its rejection of conventions to the limit. Clients face each other around a central counter that is formed by the articulation of three planes: a transparent half-moon, a translucent trapezoid in glass, and an opaque trihedral. The clarity of these materials over the luminous tiles of the floor makes them float and lessens their angularity. It also permits the client to appraise the whole of the tableau vivant composed by the customers. The light that floods the scene condemns the service area to hide behind a screen near the counter.

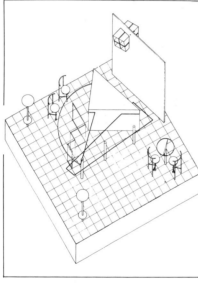

COCTELERIA 33

The Cocteleria 33 bar in Barcelona extends towards the back in two narrow counters that face each other. These are isolated from the bar by a one step shift in levels and by a smooth mirror panel reflecting the roughness of the lateral walls.

ARNOLFINI (Great Britain)

In the bar of the Arnolfini center in Bristol, a long counter in black terrazzo undulates. It is supported alternately by a short curved wall and by a metallic base on which appear drawings of hands and faces—motifs that are echoed by the countertop. Behind it, the bottles and glasses are backlit through a luminous, sanded glass wall. A row of spotlights lights the counter.

AQUYLONE

A bar can be simply treated as an element of the furniture, in the manner of a sideboard. This is the case with the sculpture/counter of Aquylone in Reggio Emilia. It presents, as if at an arm's length, superimposed metal trays held, almost balanced, by steel rods stuck in the ground. The composition is lit by the light from a yellow torch set in a casing in the ceiling.

* Cf. Visual Overview.

TO THE RESTROOMS!

Everyone goes there for the same reasons; the sign on the door confirms it. If customers like to position themselves in full view in the main room, they tend to be more discreet when they leave their seats to go to this spot. "The final circle of hell"—as Roger-Henri Guerrand wrote in his book on the history of restrooms—"is often reached by a descent to the 'W.C.' of a cafe. Every time one tries to flush, one's feet get soaked, it's backed up, they've run out of everything, it's dirty, it smells. One rarely exits unharmed from these damned places that at times are even placed near tables because space is so expensive." But, what used to be just a foulsmelling corner in most bars, often poorly lit, is being transformed into architectural spaces, treated with as much care as the bar or terrace of the cafe. The materials and the functional elements no longer conjure up classical bathroom clichés. The space is treated in the same style as the cafe, whether it be in the floor coverings, the wall coverings, or the lighting. Heavily encumbered with physical constraints, the restrooms are often in the basement. If it is impossible to avoid this, the stairs may at least be treated like those found in certain places reserved for nightlife: violent or extremely filtered lighting, little lights inset in the steps, On the axis of the descent or along the sides (as in the famous Cafe Costes by Philippe Starck), lowered ceilings, etc. Thanks to architectural efforts guided by a subtle process of amelioration, this place is gaining some nobility: as a result there's "the loo"; if you don't go there you're missing something!

CAFE COSTES[1] (France)
In the basement of Cafe Costes, glass partitions set out like a fan serve as sinks. The water comes out of a chrome tube over a barely inclined glass sheet.
1. Built in Paris in 1985 by Philippe Starck.

MIMI LA SARDINE
The metallic columns that light the restrooms at Mimi la Sardine are treated like masks, as they are in the main room. Lacquered skirting-boards line the walls, the arc shape of the mirrors is inspired by the bays in the dining room, and the broken lines of the black table detach themselves from the wall, evoking a jagged-tooth image on the plane.

CAFE BEAUBOURG
The restrooms of Cafe Beaubourg are in the basement. A curved staircase leads to an egg-shaped room. The rough stone of the arches shoulders the smooth, shiny material of the tiling (green granite from Portugal and white marble from Tassos), the mirrors, and the partitions. On the women's side, panels forming a thick cabinet serve as dressing tables. Sanded glass tiles attenuate the glare of the lamps and diffuse an appeasing light.

NICK HAVANNA * (Spain)

At Nick Havanna, the eloquent position of the masculine and feminine figures evoking pre-colombian images that are engraved on the opaque glass doors is decidedly unambiguous. The perennial white porcelain and traditional sink make way for the materials that appear in the dining room (industrial floor finish, glass, and metal) and original furnishings. The full-length mirrors enlarge the spaces and multiply the angles of vision. Veritable works of design, the sinks and faucets are treated like stainless steel and chrome sculptures; fixed to the mirror wall and to the floor, they stand, legs apart and head down. Each toilet is protected by a glass door, also opaque, which hints at the silhouettes behind it. On the men's side, serving as a urinal, a sheet of water runs down the wall, sectioned off by stone slab partitions plated in steel.

MANIN

In Tokyo, at Manin restaurant, a thread of water runs from a chrome faucet onto a marble semi-circle. A blue glass wall behind it reflects an identical slab, slightly incurved.

BAR LUCCHINO

At Bar Lucchino, the underlighting of the clear basin projects a dark circular shadow like the mirror over the glass table. As well as facilitating the upkeep, the chrome and the glass (also used in the appointments of the bar itself and of Cafe Oxy) leave no place for impurities or disorder.

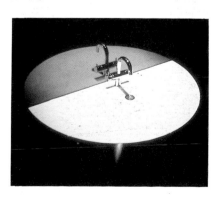

* Cf. Visual Overview.

BELGIUM 1937–1986
L'Archiduc.
6, rue Antoine Danseartstraat, 10000 Brussels.
Client: Jean-Louis Hennart.
Decorator: Pierre Bourgeois.
Located near the stock market, this old temple of 1950's jazz was redecorated in 1986 by the new owner and his decorator, with great respect for the original furniture and decor.

JAPAN 1977
Cafe Ingot.
Route 10, Kita-Kyushu.
Architect: Shoei Yoh.
Posed on a slice of land in the middle of trees, this long glass and metal parallelepiped is "balanced" on a truncated spine. One enters through a breach in the facade of reflective glass (opaque by day, transparent by night). From the exterior to the furniture, everything is in glass.

AUSTRIA 1970–1974
Kleines Cafe.
Vienna.
Architect: Hermann Czech.
In this Viennese cafe, the first intervention was to place mirrors facing each other so that the walls, bordered by wood molding, would reflect ad infinitum. In the adjacent room, mirrors placed on the lower part of two facing walls, punctuated by pillars more or less evenly spaced, reveal a subtle game on the variations in scale.

SPAIN 1979
Frankfurt Serinya.
Serinyà, Girona.
Architects: Lluis Pau/Martorell, Bohigas, Mackay.
The architects did not want to work against the spatial constraints of the renovated space (3.10 meters wide by 3.90 meters high with only one exposure in the facade). On the contrary, they emphasized the depth with two long neon tubes and a bar (white marble top, finished in white ceramic) that regroups all the functional elements of the cafe.

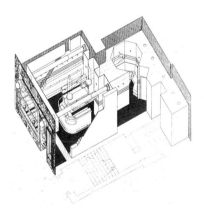

AUSTRIA 1977
Reiss Bar.
Marco-d'Aviano-Gasse 1, Vienna 1.
Architect: Coop Himmelblau.
This champagne bar was conceived as an exercise in style on the theme of a fault. In this long room, two enormous steel pistons reinforce the tension of the image while, along the walls, the broken line of a fault draws a shadowy path underlined by the shiny metal contours.

SPAIN 1979
Sukursaal.
Calle Argentina 37, Barcelona.
Architects: Dani Freixes & Vicente Miranda.
In respect for the original architecture of this restaurant situated in a rehabilitated building, the architects focused their interventions on the lighting. Garlands of lights—made of rods on which the bulbs are placed—cross the space in broken lines and are multiplied in the mirrors placed high on the walls.

UNITED STATES 1977
Museum Cafe.
Museum of Fine Arts, Boston.
Architects: I.M. PEI & Partners.
On the ground floor of the museum, a cafe space has been set up under the overhang of one of the great passages above. It has been treated like an outdoor terrace bathed in light; high poles, encrusted with vertical mirrors, become a metaphor for shady trees.

MEXICO 1979
Discoteca Magic.
Acapulco, Gro., Mexico.
Architects: Grupo LBC (Alfonso Lopez Baz, Javier Callera, Raul Rivas, Carlos Artigas).
The project called for a dance floor visible from all sides, but whose entrance would be shrouded in mystery and surprise. On the exterior, a sheet of water reflects the building. A narrow passage leads to a bridge from which one overlooks the whole space. The result combines a traditionally Mexican shape— the pyramid—and a thoroughly modern concept for the interior.

SPAIN 1983
Bar Bijou.
Calle Luis Antunez 24-25,
Barcelona.
Architect: Tonet Sunyer, Gabriel Ordeig.
The Bijou bar offers itself to passersby
like a jewelbox in the city. The warm tint of
wood dominates. The glass impost above
the door reflects the bi-colored ridges in
the building across the street. In a sophisticated manner, the rows of brick answer
the motif in the framing of the window.

FRANCE 1985
Cafeteria Casino.
Promenade des Anglais, Nice.
Architect: Jean-Michel Wilmotte.
For several years now, Jean-Michel
Wilmotte has been responsible for the
image of the Casino group's restorations.
In an old movie theatre on the
Promenade des Anglais, he was the inter-
preter for the spirit of the place, multiply-
ing, within a strict budget, the nautical
references: bulwarks, footbridges, port-
holes, buoys, etc.

SPAIN 1984
K.G.B.
Alegre de dalt 55, bajos
Barcelona.
Architect: Alfredo Vidal Alvarez.
The Kiosque General de Barcelona is a
reference, not without a certain irony, to
both the New York style of post-industrial
rehabilitation of buildings and to a sort of
"punk" aesthetic—steel structures and
metallic stairs. The lower level of the
place is the theatre for "happenings,"
where fashion, the plastic arts, and music
meet and organize themselves around a
mobile, translucent bar.

GREAT BRITAIN 1985
Le Champenois.
Cutlers Arcade, 10 Devonshire Square,
London EC2.
Architects: Julyan Wickham & Assoc.
In this basement space, lit by a cupola,
the long, sinuous bar emphasizes the
cavities and multiplies the visual axes of
the consumers. Because the dining room
is a step higher than the bar, the drinkers
and the diners are actually seated at the
same height.

ITALY 1984
Canoviano.
Via Hoepli n° 6, Milan.
Architect: Alberto Colombi.
Under the white light of a cradle-shaped
skylight, a side table marks the area
reserved for service. Multiplied infinitely
by a play of mirrors, a peristyle organizes
the table space. The marble of the floor
is echoed in the trompe-l'œil paintings on
the walls and the columns.

SPAIN 1986.
Nick Havanna.
Barcelona.
Architect: Eduard Samso.
As the owner has had a rather tumul-
tuous life (Cuban immigrant installed in
Barcelona after a few years spent in
Miami), Eduard Samso conceived a bar
made up of winks at his client's past—
borders of red stars, the front of the
counter covered in cowhide like the
Frenesi stool tops—as well as other
material effects: raw concrete floor, metallic furniture structures and brilliantly lit
screens.

AUSTRIA 1985
Bogen 13.
Innsbruck.
Architects: Reinhardt Honold, Wolfgang
Pöschl.
This jazz bar deliberately searched for a
tough location in an inhospitable part of
town, under a railroad viaduct. The inside
is so jarring as well that some policemen,
once called in on account of an uproar,
thought the place had been completely
ransacked.

UNITED STATES 1986
Kate Mantilini.
9101 Wilshire Boulevard, Beverley Hills,
CA 90210.
Architect: Morphosis.
In Beverly Hills, an old bank was con-
verted into a "steak house of the future,
on the side of a road, with a clock." By su-
perimposing a new structure on the old,
the architects created a spacious area
(with a double height) under a navy blue
ceiling with a constellation of light points,
like open sky. At the back of the restaurant stands a gigantic statue under an
oversized oculus, a symbol of solar movement and time.

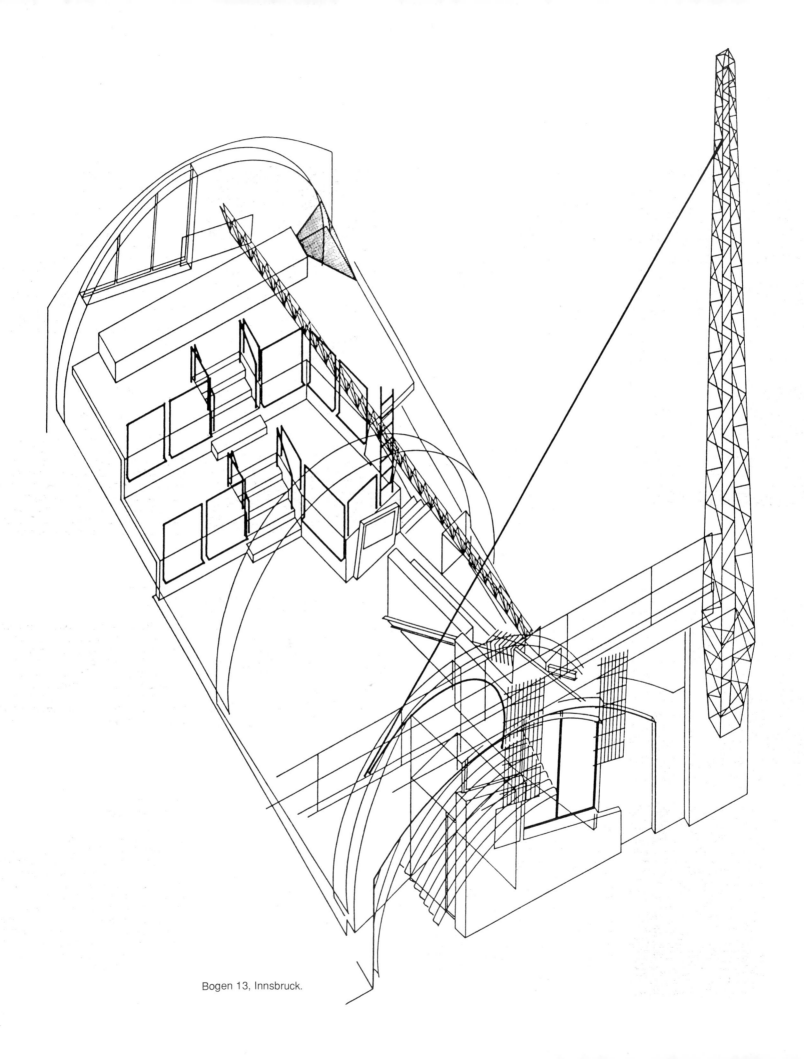

Bogen 13, Innsbruck.

FRANCE 1986
Cafe Latin.
Quai De Gaulle, 83150 Bandol.
Architect: Rudy Ricciotti.
The project was to recreate in this old seaside hotel a resort style architecture, balancing constraints of time, budget, and a local know-how that was resistant to modernity. From the lower room done in green marble, one takes a narrow stairway shaped like a footbridge to reach the upper room. The curved substructure and slightly oxidized steel balustrade (appearing as though rusted by the sea) evoke the deck of a ship.

GREAT BRITAIN 1986
Way In, Harrods Dept.
London.
Architect: Jiricna/Kerr Assoc., Future Systems.
Inside the famous London department store, the space reserved for young people—Way in—is a good example of the image of design in the 1980's. Panels in aluminum steel (under a ceiling of tubes in the same material) delimit the space of the bar. The counter in perforated metal and the white Vitralux table tops stand out against a black granito floor.

FRANCE 1986
Cafe Littéraire.
Centre national des Lettres, 53, rue de Verneuil, 75007 Paris.
Architect: Canal.
The ground floor of the entrance pavilion of an 18th century private hotel shelters a cafe conceived in the manner of a club. Inside, the shark fin cutout of the ceiling is echoed in the shape of the bar counter. Fluted panelling covers the walls. The brass picture lamps—a hint at libraries—are turned towards the tables; they draw a halo of light on the bright colors of the Trevise stucco.

GREECE 1986
Aéroport.
Pergamou Glyfada, Athens.
Architect: Tassos Meletopoulos.
This 250 square meter hangar, with a direct view of the landing strip of the Athens airport, is entirely furnished with salvaged pieces of military planes: the bar counter is a wing, the seats are from the pilots' cabin, reactors are supporting the lighting, and on the ceiling a metal globe of the earth—sculpted by G. Lappas—faces the wreck of a helicopter.

FRANCE 1986
Cargo.
41 bis, quai de la Loire, 75019 Paris.
Architect: Patrice Taravella.
Anchored near the basin of la Villette, Cargo occupies the basement of an old warehouse. The stripped-down structure as well as the use of raw materials are the only decoration; the pleasure of mastering a sober repertory overshadows the modesty of means.

ITALY 1989
Bar Bablu.
Via Ambrogio Volpi 20, Casale Monferrato.
Architects: Carmi & Ubertis Associati.
In this little rosticceria, a central space bordered by an "L" shaped counter services small alcoves. The orthogonal design on the tiles is extended in the wainscotting. Except for the Philippe Starck chairs and the Artemide lights, the furniture was specifically made for the space.

FRANCE 1986
Myrtho.
10, rue des Écouffes, 75004 Paris.
Architect: Drago R. Mrazovac.
Over a space of three years, the idea of this cafe was conceived, matured, and realized by the actual owners of the place. The cafe-restaurant stretches over two levels: the ground floor on the street serves as a little terrace while the vaulted dining room in the basement is reached by a theatrically curved metallic stairway. In this place only the architecture marks the space—the furniture is the same as in traditional bistros.

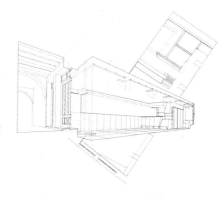

PORTUGAL 1986
Chez Lapin.
Rua dos Canastreiros, Porto.
Architect: Adalberto Dias.
This bar, having only a dozen tables and located in an old warehouse in an old part of Porto, plays a double game: effects achieved by a false ceiling, flat or oblique in the parallelepiped space, and a subtle use of materials combine the old stone of the original wall with the granite floor, marble counter, and sculpture-furniture conceived by the architect (alabaster lamps, wooden seats).

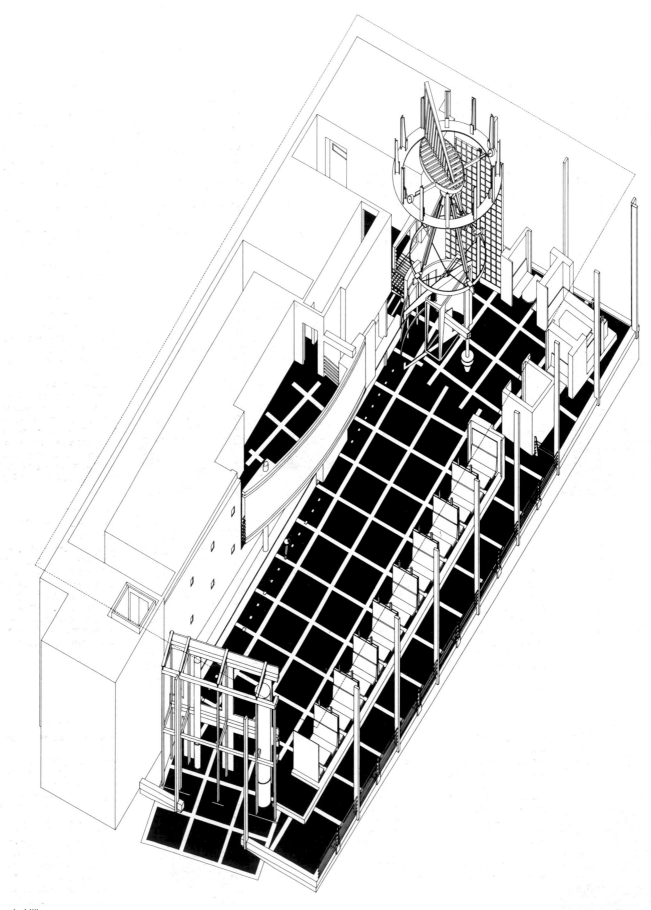

Kate Mantilini, Beverly Hills.

UNITED STATES 1987
Toscana Ristorante.
Lipstick Building, 200 East 54th Street,
New York.
Architects: Piero Sartogo & Nathalie
Grenon.
In this restaurant, the orthogonal motifs—
the Carrara marble floor, indents in the
wall appearing like Tuscan windows,
Murano glass lamps—are combined with
the curved lines of the pear tree walls
and furniture. These curves, present
even in the design of the doorknobs,
repeat the logo of the restaurant: a grand
piano.

GREAT BRITAIN 1987
New Bar and Restaurant.
Arnolfini Arts Center, 70 Narrow Key,
Bristol.
Architect: Chipperfield Associates.
Within the markedly 1960's pop
atmosphere of the Arnolfini Art Center,
the architect—in collaboration with the
artist Bruce MacLean and a limited
budget—invested primarily in the furnish-
ings of this bar-restaurant. They created
elements like the long sinuous resin coun-
ter—the motifs of which are found again
on the sanded glass panels of the bar—
and the stylized faces (which have a
1960's look) found on all the furniture.

FRANCE 1987
Cafe-Restaurant.
Gare de Plourin-Plougonven, 29216
Plougonven.
Architects: Anne Prigent & Eric
Vaiedelich.
This old railway station was refurnished
to look like a "buffet de la gare." In the
entrance axis is the bar, the result of very
subtle work on the materials of iroko and
metal. It guides the arrangement of the
restored dining rooms.

GREAT BRITAIN 1987
The Mean Fiddler.
26 High Street, Harlesden,
London NW 10.
Architects: Sean Madigan, Stephen
Donald.
The Mean Fiddler, a London space that
features all kinds of music, is made up of
a ground floor bar and a second floor res-
taurant. The "hard" atmosphere of the
first (distressed walls, a bar facade in
painted plywood and raw iron, blue
fluorescent lighting) is balanced by the
"soft" atmosphere of the latter, enhanced
by more sophisticated lighting.

FRANCE 1987
Le Paquebot.
39, boulevard du Montparnasse, 75014
Paris.
Architect: Pancho Ayguavives.
According to the architect, the curved
lines, the aluminum and ribbed steel win-
dow-breast, and the little portholes in the
metal of the facade of the Paquebot are
inspired by the drawings of Raymond
Loewy for Greyhound buses, similar to
certain Mallet-Stevens' facades or
American coffee shops of the 1950's. In-
side, the architect has combined metal
and ash burls in the furniture.

NETHERLANDS 1987
Cafe Esprit.
Address: Spui, 9 Amsterdam.
Architect: Antonio Citterio.
In Amsterdam, the branch office of the
famous Esprit company exists in an
urban historical context: it occupies a late
19th century building. The challenge was
to create a contemporary look with the
existing facade. The architect used metal
and greenhouse structures oriented to
the south.

FRANCE 1987
Puzzle.
13, rue Princesse, 75006 Paris.
Architect: Philippe Starck.
Behind a clear vitrine framed in marble, a
glass counter follows the curve of the
screen towards the kitchen. In this luxury
grocery store/snack bar—next to the
famous night-club Castel—two rooms
are superimposed, celebrating the signa-
ture style of Stark in details such as
balustrades like airplane wings and
flower vases anchored in mirrors.

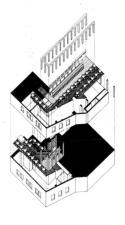

WEST GERMANY 1987
Bar Lokal.
Steinweg 1, Marburg.
Architects: Düdler/Welbergen.
The lower part of an apartment building
has been transformed into a two-level bar.
On the ground floor, the "L" shaped space
is accentuated by a strictly rectilinear bar
and has the effect of parallel streets stag-
gered with pillars. On the upper part of
these street-like spaces, little square
luminous windows underline the quasi-
urban perspective of the space. A stair-
way perpendicular to the bar, distinctly put
in perspective, leads to the upper level.

BIBLIOGRAPHY

BOOKS

Nuevos restaurantes. Justus Dahinden and Günther Kühne. Barcelona: Gustavo Gili S.A., 1974.

Ristorante. Giampiero Aloi. Milan: Ulrico Hoepli, 1972.

Googie Fifty Coffee Shop Architecture.

Excellent Shop Design, n. 28. Japan: Shotenkenchiku-Sha Co. Ltd., 1986; n. 30. Japan: Shotenkenchiku-Sha Co. Ltd., 1987.

American Restaurants II. Gen Takeshi. Japan: Shotenkenchiku-Sha Co. Ltd., 1987.

Seven Designers for Shops. Japan: Rikuyo-Sha Publishing, Inc., 1986.

French Dishes and Restaurants. Gen/Takeshi/Saito.

Créer dans le créé. Paris: Electa Moniteur, 1986.

City, le guide des villes du monde. Paris: Rivages/City, 1987.

Memphis. Barbara Radice. Milan: Electa, 1984.

Ettore Sottsass Jr. Gilles de Bure. Rivages, 1987.

Tadao Ando. Monographie. Paris: Electa Moniteur, 1982.

Adolf Loos. Liège: Ed. Pierre Mardaga, 1985.

Les Cafés littéraires. Gérard-Georges Lemaire. Paris: Henri Veyrier, 1987.

Quelques cafés italiens. Patrick Mauriès. Paris: Quai Voltaire, 1987.

Les Lieux, Histoires des commodités. Roger-Henri Guerrand. Paris: La Découverte, 1986.

Cafés de Paris. François-Xavier Bouchart. Die bibliophilen Taschenbücher, n. 284. Dortmund: Harenberg Kommunikation, 1981.

Im Café, von Wiener Charme zum Münchner Neon. René Zey, Georg Heichinger, Dieter Sawatzki. Die bibliophilen Taschenbücher, n. 521. Dortmund: Harenberg Kommunikation, 1987.

Cahiers du CCI, n. 2. "Design actualités fin de siècle." Paris: éditions du Centre Pompidou-CCI, 1986.

Restaurants, Architectur und Ambiante. Egon Schirmbeck. Callwey/Hatje.

9 H Gallery. Architectural Press Book.

JOURNALS

AMC, March 1984, June 1984, October 1984, December 1984, March 1985, October 1985, December 1985, March 1987, October 1987.

Architecture d'aujourd'hui, September 1980, September 1982, February 1984, June 1985, September 1985, June 1986, September 1986, December 1986, April 1987, June 1987, September 1987, October 1987.

Architecture intérieure-créé, November/December 1982, April/May 1986, October/November 1986, February/March 1987, October/November 1987.

Vogue décoration, April 1986.

Décoration internationale, September 1987, December/January 1987–1988.

Progressive Architecture, March 1987.

Architectural Record, August 1987, September 1987.

Architectural Review, April 1982, April 1983, February 1985, June 1986, September 1986, November 1987.

Designer's Journal, April 1986, April 1987.

Interior Design, January 1985, March and July 1987.

Ribaj Interiors, November 1986.

De Diseño, n. 5, n. 12.

Spazio e Societa, n. 24, Sansoni/Milan (December 1983).

Casa Vogue, September 1987.

Interni, n. 372 (July/August 1987).

Abitare, n. 261 (January/February) 1988.

Domus, n. 687 (October 1987).

Bauwelt, n. 43.

Werk, n. 3 (March 1985).

Wettewerbe, n. 64-65 (June/July 1985).

PHOTOGRAPHY CREDITS: *Arnold Amsler, pp. 105–107; Gert von Bassewitz, pp. 19, 20 (1), 23; Bergamo & Basso, pp. 42, 43; Bildarchiv d'Öst. Nationalbibliothek, p. 20 (2); Tom Bonner, pp. 45–47; Wulf Brackrock, pp. 11–13; Richard Bryant, pp. 63–65; Robert Burley and Tony Belcher, pp. 25–27; Lluis Casals, pp. 29–31; Robert César, pp. 56, 57; Peter Cook, pp. 66, 67; Stéphane Couturier, pp. 53–55; Sergio Dahó, pp. 35–37; Reynald Eugène, p. 99; Ferran Freixa, pp. 32, 33; Alistair Hunter, p. 69; Jean-Marie Monthiers, pp. 59–61; Gianguido Palumbo, p. 75; P. Pellion di Persano and Eddy Buttarelli, pp. 77–79; Harald Schönfellinger, pp. 21, 22; Shinkenchiku, pp. 92, 93; Yoshio Shiratori, pp. 81–85; Keiichi Tahara, pp. 87–89; Yoshio Takase, p. 91; Pieter Vlamings, pp. 95–97; Gerald Zugman, pp. 15–17; TDR, pp. 39–41, 49–51, 71–73, 101–103. Interview: p. 6, Albertina Graphische Sammlung, Christian Lutz-Sorg; p. 8, Photam, TDR.*

A Technical Issue: pp. 108–109, Richard Bryant, Yoshio Takase, Alain Le Nouail, Lluis Casals, Peter Cook, Miro Zayvoli, TDR; pp. 110–111, Stéphane Couturier, Jordi Sarra, Yoshio Takase, Keiichi Tahara, TDR. Visual Overview: pp. 112–113, Roger Begine, Hermann Czech, Steve Rosenthal, R. Camprubi, Ferran Freixa, Robert César, Tom Bonner, TDR; p. 115, TDR; p. 117, Alain Le Nouail, Peter Cook, Erminio Bottura, TDR.

Achevé d'imprimer
sur les presses
de MAME IMPRIMEURS, à Tours
N° d'impression : 23847
Dépôt légal : février 1990
Photogravure Bussière Arts Graphiques